Teaching Words and How They WORK

Teaching Words and How They WORK

SMALL CHANGES for BIG VOCABULARY RESULTS

Elfrieda H. Hiebert

TEACHERS COLLEGE PRESS
TEACHERS COLLEGE | COLUMBIA UNIVERSITY
NEW YORK AND LONDON

557 Broadway, New York, NY 10012

Published simultaneously by Teachers College Press, 1234 Amsterdam Avenue, New York, NY 10027 and Scholastic Inc., 557 Broadway, New York, NY 10012.

Copyright © 2020 by Teachers College, Columbia University

SCHOLASTIC and associated logos are trademarks and/or registered trademarks of Scholastic Inc.

Figure 7.2 images courtesy of the following:
    Portrait of Leopold Mozart, Wolfgang Amadeus Mozart, and Maria Anna
        Mozart by Louis Carrogis Carmonelle.
    Marriage of Figaro, ©Florida Grand Opera, Flickr. Creative Commons 2.0.
    Starling, ©2009 Indiana Ivy Nature Photographer, Flickr. Creative
        Commons 2.0.
    Music notes ©2019 Rosemarie Voegtli, Flickr. Creative Commons 2.0.

Figure 7.3 images courtesy of the following:
    Nautilus, ©2008 by Jitze Couperus, Flickr, Creative Commons 2.0.
    Math in nature, 2011, U.S. Army Corps of Engineers, Flickr.
    Golden rule, ©2008 by fdecomite, Flickr, Creative Commons 2.0.
    Fibonacci spiral created by Jahobr.

Library of Congress Cataloging-in-Publication Data is available at loc.gov

ISBN 978-0-8077-6317-9 (paper)
ISBN 978-0-8077-6318-6 (hardcover)
ISBN 978-0-8077-7814-2 (ebook)

Printed on acid-free paper
Manufactured in the United States of America

To my brother, Vic Toews,
who remains my role model for what it means to be a teacher.
Because of you, I learned the climate zones and so much more.

Contents

Preface

This book is about words in the texts that students read in schools and beyond. This is not, by any stretch of the imagination, the first book with the goal of increasing students' interest and knowledge of words. It is, however, the first book on vocabulary instruction that builds on knowledge from the digital revolution. The rapid processing and big data of computers have meant a revolution in our understandings of the vocabulary of texts. Scholars are no longer limited by the tedious process of hand counting words. Now the numbers, kinds, and distributions of words from millions of texts can be established in a nanosecond. This book is the first to apply the information from digitized databases of school texts to vocabulary instruction.

The view of vocabulary learning in this book has been described as generative (meaning that students have the strategies to generate meanings of unknown words). Throughout the book, I also will refer to the view as a network or relationship approach. Each of the nine chapters in the book supports this view that words are not learned as isolated entities but in relationship to other words and the underlying concepts that they represent.

The first chapter of the book gives an overview of this approach, while the second chapter describes the view of implementation of this approach. Chapters 3 through 5 present aspects of the foundational or core vocabulary of text. This core vocabulary is powerful because of its content (Chapter 3), its morphological structures (Chapter 4), and its versatility in taking on different meanings (Chapter 5).

The core vocabulary, while important, represents only a small portion of the words in the English dictionary. Knowledge about the rare vocabulary of texts is essential for successful reading. All of the thousands of rare words that can be expected to appear in school texts and beyond cannot be taught, but students can be taught about similarities and uniqueness in the roles and types of rare words in narrative texts (Chapter 6) and informational texts (Chapter 7). The final two chapters deal with two topics about which educators ask numerous questions: text complexity and English learners.

> *Long-lasting changes in the complex contexts of classrooms are made through steady application of small changes.*

The perspective on vocabulary learning and instruction will be new to many readers. Further, the means of implementation that is recommended throughout the book also is likely to be unique. The ideas about vocabulary instruction may be revolutionary, but this does not mean that existing vocabulary practices need to be overthrown in one fell swoop. Long-lasting changes in the complex contexts of classrooms are made through steady application of small changes.

The two perspectives of this book—one on learning and the other on implementation—are rich and thought-provoking. The first two chapters are devoted to developing these views, beginning with the perspective on learning in Chapter 1 and the perspective on teaching in Chapter 2. In each of the subsequent chapters, I have used a similar structure. Each chapter begins with examples of texts with vocabulary features related to the chapter's theme. This is followed by three sections. The first section, labeled "The Evidence," presents findings from scholarship related to a feature of vocabulary in school texts.

The second section, entitled "Small Changes = Big Results," describes a teacher's choices in making small changes to implement evidence-based vocabulary instruction. The teachers' stories come from workshops that I have presented across the United States on the content of this volume. The final section, called "The Last Word," can be viewed as a short blog. It provides a venue for highlighting a concern or response to questions that have been raised in workshops on the book's content.

Acknowledgments for a book that represents a 15-year journey are numerous. To the many teachers who responded, in workshops and presentations, with enthusiasm, outstanding questions, and descriptions of their practice, I wish I could acknowledge each of you individually, but the list would consume all of the space allotted for this book. Do know that your questions and comments have aided me greatly in refining and extending this work.

My colleagues at Pearson, especially Nancy Winship and Amy Fleming, and at Scholastic, Janelle Cherrington, Janet Reed, Jeannie Hutchins, and Cynthia Rothman, were instrumental in clarifying and elaborating my ideas. I apologize to those whom I have missed on this list. There have been so many of you who have given me opportunities and asked brilliant questions.

My knowledge about vocabulary and how it functions in text draws heavily on conversations and collaborations with colleagues and friends. Bill Nagy generously has provided me with my very own advanced postdoctoral seminar that has extended well over a decade. Gina Cervetti, Judy Scott, and Amanda Goodwin have been partners who have contributed greatly to this work.

Alice Folkins, my research administrator, has conducted literally thousands of analyses of the vocabulary in texts and also supervised the massive effort of scanning and proofreading texts to make these analyses of vocabulary possible. Alice, this work wouldn't be what it is without you.

Suzanne Barchers has been a stalwart over the past 2 years, giving me feedback on each chapter in every incarnation of the book. The careful reading of the final manuscript by Leslie Hall gave me the incentive to say, "It's done!"

Jean Ward generously found a home for this volume at Teachers College Press. I have treasured Jean's collegiality and friendship over the past decade and I hope, despite the challenges created by my obsessive revisions, that the friendship will be sustained.

As is the case with all of my projects, this book reflects the nourishment that Charley provides me. To recognize Charley's love for words and precise language, I want to be clear that I am using the word *nourishment* both literally and figuratively. I am able to do what I do because of the food that you provide me and the love that you give me.

—EHH, Santa Cruz, CA

CHAPTER 1

Learning Words and How Words Work

> As the cool stream gushed over one hand she spelled into the other the word water, first slowly, then rapidly. I stood still, my whole attention fixed upon the motions of her fingers. Suddenly I felt a misty consciousness as of something forgotten—a thrill of returning thought; and somehow the mystery of language was revealed to me. I knew then that "w-a-t-e-r" meant the wonderful cool something that was flowing over my hand. That living word awakened my soul, gave it light, hope, joy, set it free!
> (*The Story of My Life*, Helen Keller, 1903)

In this passage, Helen Keller describes her epiphany as a blind, deaf child with no language, when her caretaker created an experience for her that showed her for the first time the relationship between a concept and the word that labels it. This discovery awakened Keller to a life that had been denied her. Keller's soliloquy portrays beautifully the power of language. Language allows humans to make distinctions in the social and physical world. Through written language, these distinctions can be stored and then communicated across time and vast expanses of geography. This ability to reflect and revisit the distinctions made about the world at different times and places is uniquely human. True, other species can communicate. Dolphins click and whistle. Honey bees dance. Gibbons sing and call. But only humans can read the stories written by their ancestors thousands of years ago or share their discoveries for generations to come.

At the center of language are words. Words label objects, experiences, and whatever else exists in the social and physical world. Words permit humans to comprehend or create complex phenomena such as navigational systems of satellites or stories of odysseys to the future. To quote Helen Keller (1903) once more: "Gradually from naming an object we advance step by step until we have traversed the vast distance between our first stammered syllable and the sweep of thought in a line of Shakespeare."

VOCABULARY AND TEXTS: A TWO-WAY RELATIONSHIP

The integral relationship of vocabulary to knowledge means that the breadth and depth of people's vocabularies influence their life experiences. Vocabulary knowledge is a strong predictor of comprehension of texts and success in school and beyond (Quinn, Wagner, Petscher, & Lopez, 2015; Ricketts, Nation, & Bishop, 2007; Sénéchal, Ouellette, & Rodney, 2006).

But this relationship between vocabulary and texts does not go in one direction only: Texts also affect vocabulary. Although a child's initial words are learned through oral language, and oral language continues to be a source of vocabulary development, particular concepts and their accompanying labels are unlikely to occur in the conversations of everyday life. Consider, for example, concepts about the rise of democracy in Athens or the nature and consequences of shifts in tectonic plates.

Acquiring complex concepts is fostered by experiences such as demonstrations, observations, and discussions; however, texts are a valuable source for foundational and elaborated information on numerous topics, for it is in texts that human beings traditionally have stored their knowledge, whether in the form of stone tablets or electronic bytes. For students who come from communities where exposure to the concepts of academic texts has been limited, texts can be a source of equity and opportunity (Barr & Gibson, 2013).

The relationship between vocabulary and texts, then, is reciprocal. Familiarity with the vocabulary of a text supports comprehension, while, simultaneously, texts are a primary source for gaining new vocabulary. This two-way relationship can have consequences when vocabulary instruction is not adaptive and strong, especially for students whose vocabularies are not extensive on entering school. Students with strong entry vocabularies may learn to read quickly and, through reading, extend their vocabularies. Their peers with less extensive vocabularies may be off to a slow start and then may lag even further behind in vocabulary growth because they are not gaining new vocabulary from text. This pattern has been called the Matthew effect, where the rich get richer and the poor get poorer, reflecting

Stanovich's (1986) use of a biblical refer-ence (Matthew 13:12) to describe this phe-nomenon. Stopping the cycle and ensuring access to a strong vocabulary depend on well-designed learning experiences.

> *Students can expect to encounter approximately 150,000 different words over their school careers.*

Educators are faced with a challenge, however, when confronted with the task of designing powerful vo-cabulary experiences. This challenge stems from the prolific nature of English vocabulary. English dictionaries have from 450,000 to 616,500 entries (Stevenson, 2015). When it comes to school texts, experts estimate that students can expect to encounter approximately 150,000 different words over their school careers (Zeno, Ivens, Mil-lard, & Duvvuri, 1995).

Over many decades, vocabulary instruction in English/Language Arts has highlighted small groups of target words from specific texts. In this approach, 6 to 8 words are identified from a text. These words are the instructional focus for a week (Stahl & Kapinus, 2001). The 6 to 8 words a week routine was already evident in the core reading programs of the 1940s (Gray, 1941) and remains in place in many classrooms (August et al., 2014). This method of selecting and teach-ing vocabulary has been so prominent in American reading instruction that I will refer to it in this book as the 6 to 8 weekly word approach.

An example from the text *Annie's Gifts* (Medearis, 1997) with-in a 3rd-grade core reading program (Beck et al., 2008) illustrates the 6 to 8 weekly word approach. Six words from *Annie's Gifts* are identified: *except, stomped, entertain, carefree, sipped,* and *screeching*. Why were these six words chosen from this text of 910 words, ap-proximately 45 of which are words that 3rd-graders likely have not encountered in texts previously? The rationale for selecting these words is difficult to reconcile with the theme of the story—a child grappling with a lack of apparent musical talent while living in a home of musicians. Further, several of these words—*stomped, sipped,* and *screeching*—can be explained quickly with a known synonym or phrase and are only tangentially related to the theme of the story. By contrast, words related to the theme and less easy to describe with a single synonym, such as *melodious* and *rhythm*, are not addressed. Finally, if this pace of targeting six to eight words per week is main-tained across the grades, students will be directly taught about 3,500 words during their school careers. Such instruction barely skims the surface of English vocabulary.

VOCABULARY INSTRUCTION: A FOCUS ON
RELATIONSHIPS AMONG WORDS, NOT INDIVIDUAL WORDS

This book takes an alternative viewpoint to the conventional 6 to 8 weekly word approach by focusing on the relationships among words. An emphasis on networks of words is grounded in the digital revolution that began in the late 20th century. Digitization has made it possible to quickly analyze massive numbers of words in texts. By contrast, Thorndike (1921), who published the first word book for teachers, relied on counting and tabulating words by hand. Such time-consuming procedures limited the number of texts from which the list of words was drawn and the questions that could be asked about the words.

In the age of computers, large numbers of texts can be scanned and analyzed easily and rapidly. Digital programs make it possible to instantaneously establish numerous features of the words in a text; establishing the frequency of words at different grade levels and in different kinds of texts can be accomplished with a click of a button. Similarly, once an algorithm has been identified, words with similar meanings can be clustered. Words that may not be familiar to students at a specific age can be specified. Words also can be organized by root words, making it possible to identify rich groups of words with a shared meaning.

The ability to establish multiple features of words from unlimited numbers of texts has given scholars new insights into the patterns and characteristics of words in school texts. Evidence-based criteria can be applied to selecting words and can ensure an increase in the depth and breadth of the vocabularies of all students. It is this work that provides the basis for this book.

Supporting Students in Generating Meaning of Unknown Words

The perspective of this book has been described as generative (Hiebert, 2016) because its aim is for students to be able to generate meanings of unknown words. This generative knowledge comes from instruction on the patterns and features that underlie words. All words in the dictionary cannot be taught—nor should that be the aim. Rather, the target words of instruction are selected to help students generalize their knowledge about words and concepts. When introduced to new words, students are taught how to extend knowledge of the new word to other words.

The main themes of this perspective form the basis for Chapters 3 through 7. A short summary of these themes is given in Table 1.1.

In the two final chapters, these themes are applied to specific contexts of vocabulary instruction about which teachers often ask questions. Chapter 8 looks at the role of vocabulary in assignment of text complexity and shows how text complexity systems take features such as text length and sentence length into greater account than the amount of new vocabulary, even though vocabulary has been shown to be the most important factor in predicting comprehension. This chapter shows teachers how to consider vocabulary demands of texts when selecting texts to use in their classrooms.

Chapter 9 revisits the book's themes as they apply specifically to English language learners and shows teachers how to use the special strengths of English learners, particularly how to address challenges that English vocabulary poses.

The Approach in Practice

Revisiting the vocabulary in *Annie's Gifts* (Medearis, 1997) will illustrate how words are chosen within the approach of this book. A digital analysis is used to gather information on the words in the text that are likely to be valuable for students to learn. This analysis sorts words according to the age at which they enter students' oral vocabularies, the abstractness of words, the size of words' morphological families, their frequency in written language, the semantic or meaning groups into which words fall, and the number of letters in words. All of these features have been shown to influence students' knowledge of words (Hiebert, Scott, Castaneda, & Spichtig, 2019). This analysis shows that about 45 words in *Annie's Gifts* can be expected to appear frequently in future texts and may not be well known by many 3rd-graders.

A computer cannot create the semantic map (Figure 1.1) of critical words in both *Annie's Gifts* and future texts—at least not yet! But, as the map in Figure 1.1 shows, the potentially challenging words are connected semantically to the story content. The number of words in the map is almost six times the number recommended for this story in a core reading program (Beck et al., 2008). Further, when morphological family members of words like *entertain* and *performance* are addressed, the volume of words covered in instruction increases even more.

Table 1.1. Teaching Words and How Words Work: Themes

Chapter	Theme
3. Why a Small Group of Word Families Is So Important	A relatively small portion of English vocabulary—approximately 6,000 words—accounts for 90% or more of the words in school texts. These words can be clustered into 2,500 families with shared root words—families that are called word or morphological families. These words and their families matter.
4. A Short History of English and Why It Matters	Morphological families are of three types, depending on the language of origin of the root word: Anglo-Saxon, French/Latin, or Greek. Knowing how words are related in these three systems can support students when they encounter unknown words.
5. Recycling and Remixing: Multiple Meanings and Uses of Words	Many English words are versatile in their meanings and roles. Two prominent ways in which meanings of words change are through: (1) recycling, where the same word takes on different meanings, and (2) remixing, where new word meanings result from combining words and word parts. This chapter shows teachers how to help students notice and understand these processes of recycling and remixing words.
6. The Vocabulary Networks of Narrative Texts	The rare vocabulary in narrative texts supports the development of narrative elements such as the traits and behavior of characters or the events or situations that create problems for characters. In describing characters, contexts, and problems, authors typically draw on words from synonym networks to keep the narrative interesting. This process increases the number of infrequently appearing words. This chapter shows teachers how to use known words in different synonym groups to help students learn new words.
7. The Vocabulary Networks of Informational Texts	The rare vocabulary in informational texts is connected around themes. Words within these networks cluster around concepts, and the meanings of words in a network are connected but not synonymous with one another. This chapter offers ways for teachers to give students tools to acquire networks of concept vocabulary, to learn recurring academic text vocabulary, and to gain confidence with informational texts.

Figure 1.1. Semantic Map of Target Words from Annie's Gifts

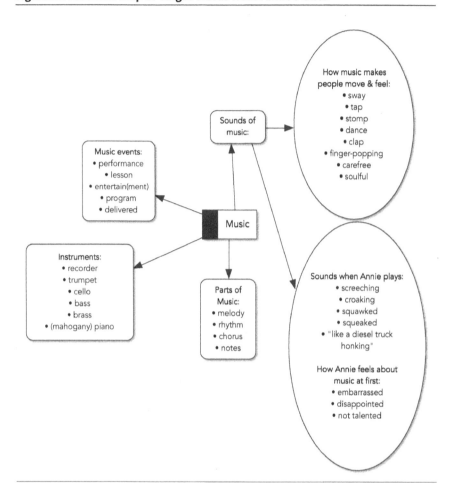

Making connections among the meanings of words in *Annie's Gifts* is only the first step of instruction. The words in Figure 1.1 are grist for teaching other features of words. Specific words in the map become the basis for creating word or morphological families (e.g., *embarrassed: embarrassment, embarrassingly; melody: melodious, melodiously*).

Words that are related to a topic but not in the story can be added to the semantic map, such as words for other instruments (e.g., *guitars, violins, saxophones*) and words related to musical performances (*recital, rehearsal*). Another lesson might deal with figurative language, including the metaphor of how Annie's piano playing sounds (like the honking of a diesel truck) and the sounds produced when Annie attempts to play different instruments. Several words in the semantic map provide excellent opportunities to discuss the presence of multiple meanings (e.g., *program, lesson*) and also multiple pronunciations of words (e.g., *bass, record*).

Through these lessons, students acquire new labels for objects and concepts, as well as new ideas about how words work. To ensure success as strong, independent readers, students must know more than the definitions *of* words; they must grasp the concepts *behind* words.

HOW TO IMPLEMENT NEW VOCABULARY INSIGHTS: SMALL CHANGES = BIG RESULTS

The benefits of teaching networks of words, rather than the 6 to 8 weekly word approach, are apparent from the many words and concepts that appear for a single story in Figure 1.1. When relationships among words are emphasized, students are exposed to many more words than when one word is taught, then the next, and so on. That exposure also connects the words that they are learning, making it easier for the brain to incorporate the new words. At the same time, students are acquiring knowledge about topics, such as musical instruments in the case of *Annie's Gifts*. Further, students are developing a stance toward vocabulary that leads them to expect that the words and ideas will be related to one another in future texts.

The ideas are clear and the advantages of the approach are evident. But when practices have been in place for a long time, as has been the case with the 6 to 8 weekly word approach, inertia often can be hard to dislodge. The network approach to vocabulary learning within this book may involve a sizeable shift in how teachers think about words, but implementing these ideas is best done through initiating small changes rather than a complete revamping of curriculum or instruction. The study of how new ideas are implemented to ensure the desired effects has been extensive over the past 30 years. The incentive for this research has been the rapid changes in the world created by technological advances. The message from this work is that steady change in educational practices is the most enduring (Bryk, Gomez, Grunow, & LeMahieu, 2015; Lang, 2016).

Making Small Adjustments

A small adjustment in instruction, such as making visible to students the connections between words related to musical instruments in a text, can influence students' learning. In turn, the success of a small change can be the incentive for both teachers and students to make more, subsequent small changes as they see big results. In so doing, teachers are equipping their students with the vocabularies they

> *Students can learn to use text itself and its initially new vocabulary to acquire the background knowledge needed to comprehend the rest of the text.*

need in order to be creators and contributors in the 21st century. Chapter 2 further develops the elements of the small change perspective. These elements are seen in the chapters that follow, along with small change implementation examples at the ends of the chapters, taken from classroom teachers and practical change examples of four kinds:

- Conversations
- Collections of words
- Core reading
- Choice reading

After all, without applications in classrooms, new insights about vocabulary are for naught.

Connections to Downloadable Resources

A special feature of this book is its direction to specific free downloadable resources like semantic maps, vocabulary clusters, and sample texts, available at the author's highly regarded website, TextProject. org, which is used by thousands of teachers. This book offers guidance on how teachers can use these materials in the classroom to grow vocabulary and understanding.

THE LAST WORD

The ideas presented here represent a transformation in views of vocabulary and how it is taught and learned. In this approach, individual words continue to be emphasized in texts of core instruction and extension activities such as choice reading. However, this book shows how both the texts and the words within these texts can be chosen carefully to ensure that students acquire fundamental knowledge about shared features and uses of words. Such knowledge gives students the capacity to grapple with the thousands of unknown words that they are likely to encounter across their lifetimes of reading. Students can learn to use text itself and its initially new vocabulary to acquire the background knowledge needed to comprehend the rest of the text. To paraphrase the adage about the effects of giving people fish versus teaching them to fish, teaching students a handful of the rare words in a single text may aid them in comprehending that text but, without knowledge about relationships across words, students will not be equipped to deal with unknown words in new texts.

What is essential to keep in mind is that students' learning vocabulary is not in itself the end goal. Instruction in the relationships among words and how words work always occurs in the service of supporting students in gaining knowledge about the world in which they live.

CHAPTER 2

Making Small Changes in Vocabulary Instruction

Example 1: Danielle's Small Change: I am going to talk about the morphological family of a word in the core vocabulary each day for a month.

vague

Example 2: Mary Ellen's Small Change: I will use one of the 20 words in
the Time unit of Word Pictures daily. After morning recess, I will hold a
short conversation about the day's word, asking students to use the word
in sentences and to write words related in meaning and morphology on
sticky notes that they put on the word wall. On the 21st day, we will tally
the number of related words and record it on our vocabulary growth
chart.

specific

Mary Ellen and Danielle were teachers in a seminar on the contents
of this book. Each committed to making a small change over a month.
Can small changes in vocabulary learning make a difference to students' learning? The answer from research is a resounding yes! Conscious attention to words can boost students' knowledge of specific
words and of how words work overall. Further, small changes can
provide the basis for additional shifts in instruction and students'
learning.

The process of making small changes, however, matters greatly. Reread the two examples that open this chapter. Think about the
changes the teachers plan to make. When statements are vague and
ambiguous, such as Danielle's, the likelihood that the small change
becomes part of classroom life is doubtful. By contrast, the specificity
of Mary Ellen's small change makes it likely to be implemented and
sustained.

The focus of this book is on relationships among words and patterns
of word use. To support the implementation of this view in practice,
each chapter includes a section called Small Changes = Big Results.

The perspective of small changes as the mechanism for implementing the ideas about vocabulary reflects recent research on how people learn and how they build new patterns of learning (Duhigg, 2014; Dweck, 2013; Gladwell, 2006; National Research Council, 2000). This chapter uses that research to describe the whys, whats, and hows of the small change perspective.

SMALL CHANGES = BIG RESULTS: WHY

The tactic of implementing small changes differs from many initiatives in education that call for substantial and rapid changes. Often, large-scale initiatives such as the No Child Left Behind Act (2002) and the Common Core State Standards (CCSS) (National Governors Association Center for Best Practices & Council of Chief State School Officers [NGACBP & CCSSO], 2010a) do not have the desired outcomes. The changes in these large-scale initiatives can be so many that they are impossible to integrate into classroom practice or are open to misinterpretation on the part of practitioners.

The Trap of Unattainable Goals

The goals of large-scale policy initiatives in literacy are not necessarily reasonable. Policymakers often have set goals in mandates that are referred to as aspirational, meaning that they are not necessarily grounded in evidence. For example, the writers of the CCSS (NGACBP & CCSSO, 2010b) recommended the acceleration of text levels across all grades to ensure that 12th-graders would be proficient with college-and-career texts. This set of levels, resembling a staircase progression, was based on a hypothetical model (Williamson, Fitzgerald, & Stenner, 2013). That is, the projections were not based on data that showed the kind of instruction required to bring all students at a grade band to a particular level. Nor was there proof that the projected increases across the grades would guarantee proficient college-and-career reading.

The Beauty of Attainable Goals

The presence of unattainable goals can lead to discouragement, disempowerment, and disengagement on the part of teachers and students. Attainable goals can have the opposite effect. Even small positive movement toward a target can be a source of satisfaction, confidence, and engagement. The small change perspective can influence teachers' views of their control over their instructional contexts. There is much in public education that causes stress and worry, such as mandated and frequent testing. Sustaining student engagement in a world where students are used to the immediacy of social media and technology adds challenges for teachers. When teachers make small changes and see that these can improve their students' engagement and knowledge, their agency as teachers can increase.

SMALL CHANGES = BIG RESULTS: WHAT

The "what" of small changes for big vocabulary results is organized around four already-established classroom practices, or the 4Cs:

- Conversations
- Collections of words
- Core reading
- Choice reading

> *Conversations are the means whereby crucial words and features of words are made visible to students.*

Conversations

During conversations, teachers make explicit the principles about how words work. In these conversations, students can engage with one another and the teacher about the application of principles. For example, a conversation might revolve around the reminder, "Every text you read has many different words. But many of the words in a text are connected by a theme." Or, after reading a text, the teacher might ask, "What were words that the author used to create a sense of doom and foreboding in the first three pages of the story?" Conversations are the means whereby crucial words and features of words are made visible to students.

Collections of Words

Collections can be thought of as word walls focused on specific features and about which students collaborate with teachers. Making additions to collections of words offers students a chance to apply their understanding of words and also gives teachers evidence regarding students' word knowledge. Contributing to collections involves much more than copying words or excerpts of words from texts. Students' selections for collections derive principally from their reading but also reflect their observations of language use outside of school and in classroom interactions. Further, students' contributions to collections give teachers grist for conversations and core instruction, where words and big ideas about words are discussed and revisited.

Core Reading

In core reading, teachers select texts that illustrate specific uses of vocabulary. These understandings of specific words are intended to support the comprehension of the text that is the focus of study. At the same time, instruction is designed to support students in understandings about vocabulary that extend across texts. For example, a short story such as "Paper" (Gagné, 2011), in which a grandmother fascinates a bored child with her skill at origami, might be chosen for its metaphors, such as the use of *choreography* to describe the grandmother's movements or the description of the child's visit to his grandmother's home as *forced confinement*. Or a story such as *Wolf!* (Bloom, 1999), in which the roles of typical fables are reversed (the farm animals are literate and unafraid; the wolf is hesitant), might be chosen to discuss irony.

Choice Reading

Choice reading refers to independent reading, a time when students read to enjoy and learn. Although choice reading is essential for a number of reasons, in relation to vocabulary development, choice reading supports a phenomenon called incidental word learning (Nagy, Anderson, & Herman, 1987). This term refers to words that are learned while reading. The style of texts is more formal than that of conversations, which means that texts often contain rare words— that is, words that occur infrequently in written language. Even in texts read to toddlers (e.g., *The Very Hungry Caterpillar*, Carle, 1994), the number of rare words can exceed those in conversations between college graduates (Hayes, Wolfer, & Wolfe, 1996). Not all new words that students encounter in texts will be remembered, but a sufficient number will be learned to accelerate students' vocabularies (Swanborn & de Glopper, 1999).

SMALL CHANGES = BIG RESULTS: HOW

Our lives as educators are hectic, both inside and outside of classrooms. A commitment, no matter how heartfelt, can go by the wayside when we are busy. To make even a small change requires structure and support. Research from social and cognitive psychology has clarified processes for building new habits or changing old patterns (B. Gardner, 2012; Lally, Van Jaarsveld, Potts, & Wardle, 2010). Systems for creating or enhancing habits share three steps: (1) defining the change, (2) identifying a specific time and place for the new practice to occur, and (3) identifying when and how to celebrate and review progress in making the change (Fogg, 2009).

Defining the Change

I begin workshops with teachers by giving a short description of the small change philosophy and inviting them to share a small change on a slip of paper at the end of the workshop. Recently, a teacher listed a small change for personal development alongside her professional small change. I was ecstatic! But when I read the contents, I grew disappointed. Her proposed personal small change was "Stop being a sugar addict." Changing eating habits, especially with an addictive substance like sugar, is not a small change by any stretch of the imagination. This proposal for change is reminiscent of New Year's resolutions where people vow to exercise more and lose weight. But New Year's resolutions rarely persist much past the first week of January. Why? Because they are too vague and too big. Proposals to have students "read more" or "hold conversations about vocabulary" are too ambiguous to be successful. The change chosen by Mary Ellen at the beginning of the chapter illustrates the necessary specificity; the change identified by Danielle lacks precision.

Choosing an activity and category. A question that frequently comes up in discussing small changes with teachers is, "What's the best one to make?" Remember, a small change is not intended to be the ultimate solution—there is no best change. The aim of the small change process is to increase the quantity and quality of students' vocabularies over time. One successful small change leads to another, which leads to another, and so on.

Each of Chapters 3 to 9 of this volume includes a small change for each of the 4Cs (conversations, collections of words, core reading, and choice reading). These suggestions serve as a menu of choices that teachers can match to their teaching style and context. This book also offers numerous options for selecting knowledge about words, such as the core vocabulary (Chapter 3) or morphological or meaning connections (Chapter 4). My recommendation is to start with one of the 4Cs and one type of knowledge about words highlighted in Chapters 3 through 7 (e.g., the morphological families of Chapter 4, the multiple-meaning words of Chapter 5). The choice of one activity in one domain of vocabulary knowledge should ensure success in starting the small change process.

Identifying the right size for the change. The aforementioned goal of "stop being a sugar addict" is the poster child for a non-example of a small change because it's big and it's broad. At the same time, a small change that says that you'll have one less teaspoon of sugar a month is also unlikely to make a discernible difference in health. Achieving a small change involves the Goldilocks principle—not too big and not too small, but just right.

Examples of small changes are offered in Table 2.1 at the end of this chapter. These small changes are not meant to be prescriptive or interpreted as the perfect changes to make, but rather are intended to illustrate a small change for each of the 4Cs (i.e., conversations, collections, core reading, and choice reading) and the content of the book (i.e., the themes unique to Chapters 3 through 7).

Two forms of each change are provided in Table 2.1: one with a future and one with little future. Two distinctions characterize the small changes with a future from those without a future. First, the small change with a future is always explicit about when and where it will take place. Second, the promising small change also defines the content. For example, the feasible small change for core reading gives the specific words for which lessons from a free, downloadable source called Super Synonym Sets for Stories will be used, whereas the ambiguous change simply states the intention to use this resource. By identifying when, where, and what, teachers do not have to make daily choices. The choice has already been made. Now the task is to implement the activity.

Ensuring resources are available. Central to the planning process is to make certain that all materials are at hand to enact the small change.

If a teacher plans to give a talk on a book but doesn't have the book at hand, the event probably won't happen. In one of the introductory vignettes, Mary Ellen is implementing the introduction of a word a day with Word Pictures from TextProject.org. At present, the series consists of pictures for 16 topics. Without the choice of a topic (and the downloading of materials), Mary Ellen's intention may wane.

Writing it down. Nothing will happen consistently if a small change is not written down. Teachers can leave workshops (or even finish reading this book!) with the goal of "I'm going to teach students more about words." A day after the goal has been stated, the memory of exactly what was said becomes less clear and soon is forgotten. Fortunately, human beings have a scaffold to assist in remembering—written language. Teachers devote large blocks of time to supporting their students' production of written language. However, as teachers, we are often reluctant to follow our advice to students. A written plan, starting with the content of and reason for the change, is the foundation of the small change process. Reviewing the why can be essential in sustaining the effort. For example, a prominently displayed statement on a teacher's desk can keep the vision alive: "Vocabulary is the engine that drives proficiency in many domains. When students learn new words, this knowledge can be theirs forever."

Identifying a Time and Place

The small change needs to be associated with a particular time and place in a school day. Experts in the field of social change describe the need for a "cue" or a "trigger" (Fogg, 2009; Neal, Wood, Labrecque, & Lally, 2012) that signals when it is time to implement the practice. For example, if the designated time and place for the small change is right after recess on Mondays, Wednesdays, and Fridays, both teacher and students know exactly when to start the activity.

When? An often-heard complaint of teachers is that there just isn't enough time in the school day to add anything. However, researchers who have studied classrooms point to small pockets of time that can be described as "dead time" in relation to learning (Stallings, 1980). Instances of such transition times include lining up (with its concomitant pushes, shoves, shrieks, and admonishments) or getting materials ready for a new activity. Such short periods of time can be perfect for initiating small changes, especially those related to conversations

about vocabulary or collections of
words. Transitions as students prepare materials for a content area,
move from one area of the school to
another, or enter and exit the class-

> *Short periods of time can be perfect for initiating small changes.*

room (e.g., beginning and end of day, after lunch, after recess)—all of
these are potential times for initiating small changes. A small change
in a transition period also can be a useful way to orient students for
learning in the next period of the day.

How long? Just as automaticity in students' reading is critical,
teachers are aiming for automaticity in their small changes. Writers
in the literature of habit formation bandy about different numbers
as to the length of time it takes to make a small change permanent.
An often-cited number is 21 days. Others say 40 days. Recently, I saw
someone extend the prediction to 66 days (which seems like a strange
number!). Few of these estimates are based on real data.

My estimate is that the length of time required for permanent
change is a function of the content and size of the change. A change
that involves students in collecting words (where there is a concrete
outcome) may be quicker to implement than a change in core reading
(where procedures are more complex).

Teachers also should remember that they are not the only ones
who are making a change in their classrooms. If the small change requires a shift from long-held expectations or routines on the part of
students, the process is likely to take longer than a change that is integrated easily by students. Engaging students in being co-participants
in the small change will support its success. In fact, conscious participation in putting habits into place (and revising when necessary)
might be one of the most essential strategies students learn in school.
The small change process provides powerful modeling that could carry
forward into other aspects of students' lives.

Identifying the Celebration and Review

It is in the third and final part of the small change cycle that teachers
(and students) view their progress in a small change and determine
whether their undertaking requires rework or whether the project
can be declared a success. This final step has two parts: consistent celebration and periodic reviews.

Celebration. Often, the focus in education is on outcomes or goals that have not been attained. The small change perspective attends to what has been accomplished. Celebration does not wait until the end of the school year. Celebrations begin with the first implementation of the activity and extend over the course of the project. Whenever the activity is implemented as planned, the teacher and students might raise hands in the air and state, "We did it! We learned a new word today. And one word means a whole family of words. Hooray for us!" The activity might culminate with a class member putting a sticker on a chart confirming its completion for the day. When the activity does not occur for whatever reason (e.g., an unexpected school assembly), there also should be a recognition that the activity was not accomplished. Table 2.2 at the end of the chapter includes additional ideas for daily ways of acknowledgment or recognition of a small change in vocabulary learning.

Finally, when the target end date has arrived (e.g., the 20 days to which Mary Ellen committed), a larger celebration occurs. Labeling steps in enacting small changes as milestones is especially appropriate, since a milestone is a roadside marker that lists the distance to a particular landmark. When a milestone has been reached, it's time to celebrate progress on the journey!

Rather than the ubiquitous popcorn or pizza party, literacy accomplishments should be celebrated with literacy events. For example, students might make collages of new word families, which are displayed prominently in the hallway leading to the classroom. Yet another possibility would be for students to make cartoons of literal illustrations of compound words, such as a quarterback throwing a foot for *football*, similar to those in Brunetti's *Word Play* (2017). Additional ideas for milestone celebrations—the ones that recognize that the small change has been implemented successfully over the designated period of time—are included in Table 2.2.

Review. Testing, accountability, and assessment have given data gathering a bad reputation in schools. In life, however, human beings regularly use data. People know how much they weigh (especially after a holiday like Thanksgiving) and how much money will be in the bank after bills have been paid. For small changes to stick, implementation needs to be tracked, which means collecting and studying data. This tracking does not need to take the form of unwieldy Excel spreadsheets. A simple check on the calendar will do the job. A chart that is highly visible to everyone—teacher and students—can go a long way toward ensuring that the small change is enacted consistently.

Additionally, teachers should do a weekly review of progress on their small change. Even a short period of reflection gives teachers the chance to determine what has and has not been working. Real life, especially in classrooms with their many participants, does not always go according to plan. Sometimes, plans are too ambitious. Other times, the activity begins to transform and takes up time required for other tasks. Regular review and fine-tuning ensure that small changes are sustained. Reflection by students on progress (or lack thereof) also can assist them in learning how to achieve goals.

Getting Support for Making Small Changes

The very best possible scenario for change is when it is undertaken with a collaborator or as a group. Making changes in the complex contexts of classrooms can be challenging for individual teachers. Ideally, literacy coaches and instructional leaders at school sites will engage a faculty in making small changes. If schoolwide support is not available, teachers can look for partners in their district. And, when neither instructional leadership nor fellow teachers in close proximity are available, the digital age offers ways to engage support from like-minded colleagues in other geographic locales. Digital tools allow teachers who meet in a seminar, workshop, or virtual environment to become partners in the small change process.

THE LAST WORD

The implementation of the 4Cs (conversations, collections of words, core reading, and choice reading) is intended to move vocabulary learning away from the pervasive activities of worksheets, games, or definitions to engagement with words in texts. After writing this last sentence, I entered the key words *vocabulary activities* into a web browser. Well over a million websites were suggested. In the top 10 websites, the most common activities were word bingo (card has the definition and the caller gives the word), vocabulary relays (students fill in words related to a category that start with the letters of the alphabet in order), and the dictionary game (where a word is given and students need to write plausible definitions). The approach in this volume is quite different than these typical vocabulary activities in its emphasis on actions that support understanding how words connect and the systems underlying words in the context of engaging and compelling texts.

Table 2.1. Plans for Small Changes: Sustaining Power

Activity Type	Content Focus	Small Change with No Future	Small Change with a Future
Conversations	Chapter 4: A Short History of English and Why It Matters	I will lead conversations on the number of words in English, highlighting the number of rare words that students are likely to encounter.	I will conduct a mini-lesson at the beginning of the ELA period on Mondays and Thursdays for the 4 weeks of March, beginning on the first Monday of March. For each of these 8 lessons, I will use one of the 8 mini-lessons at TextProject.org on "What you already know about words . . . and what you need to know."
Collections	Chapter 7: The Vocabulary Networks of Informational Texts	I will have students collect content words from informational texts in our leveled book program.	For two 2-week periods, I will cluster leveled texts on two topics: games and nature. I will put 3–4 words that are shared in the cluster of leveled texts on the word collection at the beginning of each 2-week period. I will ask students to add words to the word collection at the end of each guided reading lesson.
Collections	Chapter 3: Why a Small Group of Word Families Is So Important	I will have students generate morphological family members for words in TextProject's Word Pictures.	I will use 4 Word Pictures (Transportation, Nature, Water, Communication), one each week, in a learning center where students add morphological family members to the target words.

Activity Type	Content Focus	Small Change with No Future	Small Change with a Future
Core Reading	Chapter 6: The Vocabulary Networks of Narrative Texts	I will do a lesson from the Super Synonym Sets for Stories each week in January.	I will focus on semantic clusters for *think, argue, observe,* and *say* (from the Super Synonym Sets for Stories) for 8 lessons, 2 per week in January. I will begin the ELA period on Tuesdays and Wednesdays with a whiteboard presentation on a word, with the Tuesday presentation focusing on multiple meanings of the words and the Wednesday presentation on the idioms and Spanish connections.
Choice Reading	Chapter 5: Recycling and Remixing: Multiple Meanings and Uses of Words	I will give book talks in October from Table 5.3 of *Teaching Words and How They Work.*	I will give one book talk on Wednesdays, right after lunch, for each week of October. I will select 4 books from Table 5.3 (Books That Illustrate the Recycling and Remixing Process) from *Teaching Words and How They Work,* each illustrating a different principle about words. After reading a section of a book, I will lead a discussion on the features of words exemplified in the book. I will put the book in a visible place in the library corner.
Choice Reading	Chapter 8: Vocabulary and Text Complexity Systems	I will teach students the five-finger rule.	I will give a mini-lesson on "Choosing the Right Book" on Mondays, right after lunch, for each week of October. During the 1st week, I will demonstrate the five-finger rule. In subsequent weeks, I will review with students the five-finger rule. I will then ask students to demonstrate how they used the rule in selecting their current book for choice reading.

Table 2.2. Examples of Daily and Milestone Celebrations in Making Small Changes

Daily Celebrations	Milestone Celebrations
Recording occurrences of a small change on a chart or calendar	Sharing artifacts and messages about new vocabulary and/or vocabulary patterns through social media
Playing a ringtone version of a song: • "I Just Want to Celebrate": Rare Earth • "We are the Champions": Queen • "Celebration": Kool and the Gang	Creating a physical representation of new vocabulary (e.g., collage, books)
Engaging in a physical action (e.g., waving hands above head)	Selecting a new trade book for a read-aloud event
Noting the number of words learned from a collection of words on a chart	Inviting another class (including a virtual visit) to a summary of vocabulary accomplishments

CHAPTER 3

Why a Small Group of Word Families Is So Important

Example 1: Startled, **Omakayas** slipped and spun her arms in wheels. She **teetered,** but somehow kept her balance. Two big, skipping hops, another leap, and she was on dry land. (*The Birchbark House,* Erdrich, 2002)

Example 2: The mountain seemed much the same as it had been for the past month. Suddenly, at 8:32 a.m., Mount St. **Helens erupted** with incredible force. (*Volcanoes,* Simon, 2006)

Example 1 may come from a story and Example 2 from an informational text, but the two texts that introduce this chapter have something in common: The majority of the words (those in regular type) come from a relatively small group of 2,500 word families, while the words in boldface do not. Word or morphological families consist of groups of words with the same meaning unit or morpheme. For example, the family of the root word *care* has inflected endings (*cares, cared, caring*), suffixes (*careful, carefully, careless, carelessness*), and compounds (*carefree, caretaker, childcare, daycare*).

In this chapter, I address these families of words that students will encounter time and again in texts. The prominence of these 2,500 word families in written language has led me to use the term *core vocabulary* to describe them. The core vocabulary forms the bedrock for proficient comprehension.

THE EVIDENCE

The English language has a rich lexicon or vocabulary, with more words than most other languages have (Leech & Rayson, 2014; Mugglestone, 2013). The *Oxford English Dictionary,* the most definitive

> *The majority of the words (those in regular type) come from a relatively small group of 2,500 word families.*

source of English vocabulary, has well over 300,000 main entries (Stevenson, 2015). For example, the word *goal* has two main entries—one for the word as a noun and the other as a verb. Additionally, there are 326,000 sub-entries that include combinations (e.g., *goalpost*), derivatives (e.g., *goalward*), and phrases (e.g., *goal to go*). These counts, however, do not take into account the nuances in a word's meaning. The entry for *goal* as a noun shows two distinctive meanings: (1) something someone wishes to achieve in the future and (2) making a ball/object go into a particular area to win a point in a game or sport. Even though these two meanings are used in distinctive ways, they appear under the same entry in the dictionary.

Even if only the main entries for words are considered and not multiple meanings or derivatives and phrases, using the 6 to 8 weekly word approach means that students are directly taught only a small fraction of the words in English. In the meanwhile, many new words will have entered English. Even the venerable *Oxford English Dictionary* issues a list of words that have been added to the dictionary at four different times annually. The list announced in June of 2019 consisted of 1,400 words, senses, and subentries, including *bridalware* (clothing worn by or suitable for a bride) and *twittersphere* (users of the social media application Twitter, considered collectively).

Many Words But Big Differences in Their Use

But there is good news. All words do not appear with similar frequency in English vocabulary. The words in English follow a skewed distribution, which means that a small percentage of words make up the bulk of *all* words, while the vast majority of English words occur very rarely. This pattern can be seen in Table 3.1 where a distribution of words from an analysis of school texts is presented. This analysis was based on 17.5 million total words from school texts that covered grades 1 through college and a comprehensive sampling of subject areas (Zeno et al., 1995).

In looking at Table 3.1, a distinction to bear in mind is *unique* words (different words) and *total* words (all words). In the previous sentence, there are 20 total words and one number. Since the word *in*

Table 3.1. Appearance of the Core Vocabulary Groups with Sample Words

Word zone	Predicted appearances in 1 million words	Number of words in zone	Proportion of *unique* words in sample (n = 154,941)	Proportion of *total* of 1 million-word corpus	Illustrative words
1	1,000+	107	.07	.48	the, by
2	999–300	203	.13	.1	father, last
3	299–100	620	.4	.1	pressure, behavior
4	99–30	1,676	1.1	.09	protect, balance,
5	29–10	2,980	1.9	.05	curve, emotional
6	9–1	13,882	8.9	.04	garment, inventory
7	<1	135,473	87.4	.14	nonplussed, fluorescence

Source: Hiebert (2005a) based on Zeno et al. (1995)

appears twice and *words* appears four times in the sentence, there are 16 unique words and one number.

In Table 3.1 the first group of words (called a word zone) has 107 unique words. These words are predicted to account for about 48% of all words in school texts. With the words in the next four zones (i.e., word zones 2 through 5), 82% of the total words in texts are addressed. What this means is that a relatively small portion of the English vocabulary—about 5% of the unique words—is responsible for a little more than 80% of the total words in school texts from grades 1 through college.

Identifying the Core Vocabulary

Because the vocabulary gap between the haves and the have-nots (Hart & Risley, 1995; Hoff & Tian, 2005) is great, the only way to close this gap is through an economical use of students' time in school. Over the past 15 years (Hiebert, 2005a, 2017), I have worked to determine how vocabulary can be taught efficiently. The first focus of my research was to determine whether the words in word zones 1 through 5 could be parsed more efficiently as groups of words, rather than viewing them as individual words to be taught.

The organization that I chose for grouping words is the morphological system. Therefore, a brief overview of morphology is in order. Morphology has to do with meaning units or morphemes. These units are of two kinds. The first are the free morphemes or roots that hold meaning (e.g., *amble*). Bound morphemes, the second type, do not hold meaning on their own but allow for grammatical and semantic changes in root words. Bound morphemes include inflected endings such as *-ed, -ing,* and *-s,* which change the tense of root words (e.g., *ambled, ambles, ambling*), or prefixes and suffixes such as -tory, -ance, and non-, which can change the root word's part of speech (e.g., from a verb to an adjective: *amble* to *ambulatory*) or the word's meaning (e.g., *non-ambulatory, ambulance*).

Choosing morphological families as the unit for the core vocabulary was based on evidence that even most 1st-graders understand that the inflected members of a word family (i.e., -ed, -ing, -s/es) share meaning with the root word (Anglin, 1993). Research also has shown that students can be taught to increase connections across words with shared morphemes (Goodwin & Ahn, 2010). Grouping words into morphological families, then, makes sense.

My colleagues and I (Hiebert, Goodwin, & Cervetti, 2018) found that the 5,586 most frequent words (i.e., those in word zones 1 through 5 in Table 3.1) could be grouped into 2,500 word families. When relatives for these families are added from word zones 6 and 7, there are approximately 11,300 words in the 2,500 morphological families.

To verify that this group of words does, indeed, account for the majority of words in text, we (Hiebert et al., 2018) analyzed the exemplar texts identified by the Common Core State Standards writers (NGACBP & CCSSO, 2010c). An average of 91.5% of the total words in exemplar texts from kindergarten through college-and-career levels came from the 2,500 word families. The word families within the core vocabulary have an average of 4.5 members. What this means is that to be proficient at reading English, students need to be adept at generalizing their knowledge of meaning across several different forms of a word. The role of morphology is so central to the core vocabulary—and to proficient reading of English—that Chapter 4 is devoted to it.

What 2,500 Word Families Mean for Instruction and Learning

At first, 2,500 word families may seem like a daunting number, especially from the viewpoint of conventional instruction where typically 6 to 8 words are taught over a week. Within the 6 to 8 weekly word approach, 2,500 words would require 10 years of instruction! Within a network approach to vocabulary instruction—the perspective emphasized throughout this volume—each of the 2,500 word families is not treated as a separate entity. When connections across words are fostered, numerous words—including ones not in the 2,500 word families—are taught and learned. *Annie's Gifts* (Medearis, 1997) in Chapter 1 illustrates the wide net that is cast when relationships among words, rather than individual words, are the focus of instruction. In the case of *Annie's Gifts*, the network approach means that 36 words are highlighted in a week of instruction, rather than the six words recommended in the core reading program. Once members of the families of the 36 words and their multiple meanings are included, the number of words taught in a week can triple or even quadruple.

Ensuring that students become highly automatic with the meanings of words within the 2,500 morphological families should not be a source of worry to teachers for two reasons. First, many of the words in the 2,500 word families are already in students' oral vocabularies by the time they see them in text. Children have used words such as *big, wet, dog,* and *bed* since they were toddlers. These words do not need to be taught directly but, rather, can be used to teach students new patterns and uses of words. For example, *big* and *wet* are used to demonstrate comparison words (*bigger, biggest, wetter, wettest*), while *dog* and *bed* are used to illustrate compound words (*doghouse, bulldog, bedroom, bedside*). Students' vocabularies increase rapidly as words in their oral language vocabularies are extended to family members and related words.

Second, the words in the core vocabulary do not occur all at once. About 70% of the lead words (i.e., the most frequent word) of the morphological families are predicted to appear by the end of the primary-grade period. Most of the remaining word families become apparent in middle-grade and middle school texts, and a small group becomes frequent in only high school texts.

This overview of the core vocabulary demonstrates that the 2,500 word families and their members are not words to be memorized and learned through rote practice and worksheets. Quite the contrary.

The words in the core vocabulary represent the essential ideas of the natural and social words. The members of the 2,500 morphological families also exemplify crucial principles of how words work in texts.

The 2,500 Morphological Families = Key Concepts

The meanings that words convey are ultimately why words matter. In this section, the core vocabulary is examined from two perspectives on meaning: (1) the presence of semantic or meaning-related categories, and (2) the concreteness or abstractness of words. A foreshadowing of a third aspect of meaning—multiple meanings of words—is given at the end of the section. This feature is of such consequence in the core vocabulary that Chapter 5 is devoted to this feature.

Semantic categories. Semantic clusters are categories of words with shared meanings (Jackendoff, 1992). The word *print*, for example, fits with a group of words such as *write* and *copy*. Related meanings might be *reproduced* and *published*—actions that can be substituted for the word *printed*, depending on the context. The word *bear* fits into a different kind of semantic category, Large land animals. Other members of this category, such as *buffalo, camel,* and *yak,* are not synonyms of *bear*, as is the case with words in the *print* network. Instead, each member of this semantic category represents a distinct creature.

Not all semantic networks are precisely the same, as the examples of *bear* and *print* show. Marzano and Marzano (1988) offered a database of semantic networks among 7,250 words in elementary textbooks. They developed a three-tier classification of word meanings, beginning with superclusters (e.g., literature/writing), followed by clusters within a supercluster (e.g., types of books, drawings/illustrations), and ending with miniclusters (e.g., words around writing, such as *print*).

Marzano and Marzano's (1988) classifications are highly useful, but the presence of 61 superclusters has meant that the system has not had the widespread use in schools that it merits. Consequently, I have consolidated the superclusters into 11 megaclusters (Hiebert, 2011). The supercluster for literature/writing is part of the megacluster for social systems. Other superclusters in this group are entertainment, arts, and sports.

As illustrated in Table 3.2, words from the core vocabulary are present in all 11 megaclusters. Indeed, the 2,500 morphological families are a microcosm of ideas that typically make up stories and informational texts.

Table 3.2. Distributions of Word Categories in the Core Vocabulary

Category Name	Words Within Core Vocabulary (#)	EXAMPLES WITHIN SEMANTIC CLUSTERS	
		Core Words	Core Words That Are Phonetically Regular and Monosyllabic
1. Emotions and attitudes	110	serious, happy, mad	mad, sad, glad
2. Communication	239	whispered, suggested, recommended	ask, thank, speak
3. Traits of characters and social relationships	174	sturdy, lazy, popular	weak, neat, slim
4. Characters (occupations; types of people and groups)	205	knights, herd, husband	team, club, class,
5. Action and motion	209	slipped, pace, joined	shut, chase, slide
6. Human body (including clothing)	139	teeth, membrane, jacket	skin, neck, lips
7. Features and physical attributes of events, things, people and experiences (including size/quantity, time, location/direction)	487	necessary, locked, frequently	deep, thick, flat
8 Places/events	126	shelter, restaurant, ceremony	home, shop, hut, shed
9. Natural environment	391	volcano, peninsula, pasture	leaf, tide, oak
10. Machines (including transportation, materials)	174	vehicle, motor, oil	van, jet, ship
11. Social systems (literature/writing; language; money; sports; entertainment/arts)	162	soccer, sentence, dollars	sing, read, note

The words within the 2,500 families are not necessarily the most sophisticated or precise expressions of an idea. For example, the words *angry* and *mad*, both within the core vocabulary, are part of a semantic network that includes numerous rare words such as *incensed, irate,* and *wrathful.* Beyond the primary grades, authors are likely to use the more sophisticated words in their texts. Students' exposure to frequent words such as *angry* and *mad* means that these known words can be used as a point of reference to quickly explain the meanings of the more sophisticated members of the cluster when they appear in text.

Concreteness and abstractness. An image of a *bear* can be brought to mind quickly, while the conjunction *between* does not elicit a concrete image. More than a third of the core vocabulary words represent concrete objects—words such as *bear, clouds,* and *bus.* Even if children have never seen a bear, the concept can be developed vicariously with a picture. Beginning readers frequently are introduced to reading with words such as *and, had,* and *get* because of their high-frequency status. But their abstract meanings are ambiguous for young children.

Earlier in the chapter, I described the lopsided distribution of words in English, where a very small percentage of English words—about 107 words—accounts for 48% of the words in school texts (see Table 3.1). The words in this group are called high-function or glue words because they serve to connect ideas in written language. A common view has been that since these words are so dominant in text, teaching them first will give beginning readers access to almost 50% of the words in texts. For several reasons, however, high-function words can be challenging as the first words for young children to learn.

Consider the 10 most frequent of the high-function words in written English: *the, of, and, to, a, in, is, that, it,* and *was.* These words provide valuable connections to ensure that ideas are in complete sentences. Young children who are native speakers of English are likely to have heard and used these words thousands of times in their preschool years. But most young children would be hard pressed to describe what these words mean (and many adults as well!). Further, most young children are not attending to these words when they are read or even when they speak or listen. Young children are interested in birds, bugs, and balls, and their focus is on characters and actions in a text, not the determiners or prepositions.

The abstractness of the meanings of these words can contribute to their challenge for young readers. Brysbaert, Warriner, and Kuperman (2014) have provided the ratings of many words on an abstractness–concreteness scale where 5 is most concrete (e.g., *elephant*) and 1 is abstract (e.g., *although*). The 10 most frequent words, listed above, have a rating of 1.8 on this scale, which means that they are very abstract. Abstract words are more difficult for beginning and struggling readers to remember than concrete words (Walker & Hulme, 1999).

The sound–letter relationships form a second challenging feature of the high-function words. High-function words were among the first to be written down in English centuries ago and do not represent contemporary pronunciations (Baugh & Cable, 2012). Consequently, the sound–letter correspondences, particularly for vowels, in some of these words are not the typical ones. Of the 10 most frequent high-function words, five have vowel patterns that are irregular: *the, of, was, a, to*. Taken together, these features of abstractness and unique pronunciation mean that the most frequent words in written English can be challenging for students to learn. Readers need to become fluent with high-function words, but a focus solely on these words in beginning reading, without commensurate attention to concrete words, can exacerbate challenges for some young children.

Another group of abstract words within the core vocabulary are labeled general academic words, examples of which are italicized in the following sentences from a social studies textbook: "Geography helps us *understand* our environment. An environment *includes* all the surroundings and *conditions* that *affect* living things" (Viola et al., 2009, p. 6). A social studies lesson likely will focus on the concept of the environment, not on words such as *includes* and *affect*. The general academic words rarely get the attention they deserve in either content-area or ELA instruction.

Most of the general academic words do not appear with frequency until the middle grades and beyond, where they can pose obstacles to proficient reading for some students (Cummins & Yee-Fun, 2007). The difficulty with general academic words stems from their ubiquitous nature in texts. The word *connect* receives frequent use in content areas but it also is used in directions for academic tasks (e.g., Make a connection between the two writers' styles). Since general academic words are especially relevant to informational text, they receive a more in-depth treatment in Chapter 7.

Other dimensions of word meaning. The words *bear* and *print* illustrate another important aspect of core vocabulary: They are frequent because they are versatile. The word *bear* has two distinctive historical meanings. One is as a noun—a large, heavy mammal—and the other is as a verb—to carry or bring forth. Even words such as *print*, with only one historical meaning, often serve as both nouns and verbs. And, within one part of speech, a word can have several meanings. As a noun, *print* can refer to the text or type of a publication or to a mark left on a surface.

Many of the words in the core vocabulary are core precisely because their multiple meanings lead to their frequent use. Those frequent uses in different contexts require flexibility on the part of readers. The multiple meanings of the core vocabulary will be described in more depth in Chapter 5.

The relationship between the morphological and orthographic systems. Morphological patterns are not the only critical system in written English. When students first learn to read, the sound–spelling (sometimes called phonological–orthographic) system gets the lion's share of attention, starting with an emphasis on phonics. The spelling and the morphology systems of English are not discrete. They overlap. A morphological or meaning unit has a spelling and a set of sounds associated with it. For example, the spelling and sounds associated with *add* are retained in word family members such as *adding* and *additional*. There are instances where spellings and sounds are modified to accommodate suffixes (e.g., *pronounce, pronunciation*) but the essential parts of the spelling are retained.

The way in which the sound–spelling and morphological systems interact is often forgotten in the push to develop young children's fluency with the relationships between letters and sounds. If decoding instruction emphasizes words such as *cod, cog,* and *con,* as Bloomfield and Barnhart (1961) suggested in their linguistic approach, students who are unfamiliar with the meanings of *cod, cog,* and *con* will not know whether they have been successful in their decoding efforts. Students cannot read without strong decoding skills, but, at the same time, success at decoding requires knowledge of word meaning (Ouellette, 2006; Perfetti & Hogaboam, 1975; White, Graves, & Slater, 1990).

In its focus on vocabulary, this book is not a comprehensive treatment of reading pedagogy such as the acquisition of decoding. However, becoming adept at decoding involves recognizing the meaning of a word as well as its sound–letter relationships. As the illustrations in Table 3.2 show, numerous words in the core vocabulary have consistent and common phonics patterns and belong to prolific rime groups. Rime groups consist of words that share vowel(s) and consonant(s), as in *an* and *eat*. For example, several words within the category of transportation share rimes with a substantial number of words in the core vocabulary: *van* (e.g., *can, man, ran*), *jet* (e.g., *pet, wet, met*), and *ship* (e.g., *trip, slip, lip*). Suffice it to say that there is an abundance of highly frequent, highly meaningful, and highly decodable words within the core vocabulary from which curriculum developers, publishers, and writers can create texts that foster meaningful word recognition.

Distinguishing Between Core and Rare Words

If the words in the 2,500 word families are responsible for approximately 90% of the total words in texts, that means that the remaining unique words—approximately 149,000 in school texts—appear infrequently. Rare appearances should not be equated with unimportance. The words *conglomerate, disconcerted*, and *monotone* may be quite rare (likely to appear once in every 2 million words of text) but when they do appear, they convey nuanced and distinctive meanings.

In this volume, the core vocabulary (word zones 1 to 5) is distinguished from the rare vocabulary (word zones 6 and 7). Both the core and rare vocabulary are critical foci of instruction. It is not a question of "either-or." Nor is it the case that one focus precedes the other. Both core and rare words are addressed in vocabulary instruction, beginning in the early years. However, the forms of the experiences for the core and rare vocabulary vary. The distinctiveness of the core vocabulary is addressed in this chapter and the next two (Chapter 4, "A Short History of English and Why It Matters" and Chapter 5, "Recycling and Remixing: Multiple Meanings and Uses of Words"). Rare vocabulary is treated in Chapters 6 ("The Vocabulary Networks of Narrative Text") and 7 ("The Vocabulary Networks of Informational Texts").

SMALL CHANGES = BIG RESULTS

A visit to a 2nd-grade classroom demonstrates how a teacher implements small changes to support students' facility with the core vocabulary. Joshua has chosen to focus on the core vocabulary because he

Figure 3.1. The Core Vocabulary in Mathematics Story Problems

1. There are **2** children at **each** music stand. **How many children are at 6** music stands? **What do you need to find out?**
2. There are **3** people in **each** car. **How many** people **are in 7 cars?**
3. Each dance group has **10** dancers. **How many** dancers **are in 5 groups?**

Note: Bold words are in word zones 1 to 3.

knows 2nd grade is critical in ensuring strong vocabulary recognition. He has made a small change each quarter of the school year, beginning with conversations and, subsequently, collections of words, core reading, and choice reading.

Conversations

Over a school year, Joshua talks with students about the role of the core vocabulary in text. These conversations occur especially during instruction in content areas to make students aware that the core vocabulary occurs in texts across the curriculum, not simply English/ Language Arts.   At the beginning of a math lesson on patterns, for example, Joshua projects three story problems onto a screen, as illustrated in Figure 3.1 (Greenes et al., 2005, pp. 610–611). He goes through the problems, asking students to identify the words that they know. Joshua reminds students that some words, such as *stand* and *group,* are frequent because they take on different meanings in text. He attends especially to the word *group* because, in students' prior experience with this word in mathematics, they have been asked to group objects together.

Joshua ends the conversation with a reminder: "The words you know make you power readers and you already know many of the words that will keep showing up in texts forever!" Then he asks students to give a seatmate a high five to recognize their vocabulary prowess.

Collections of Words

Joshua has found the use of the Word Pictures at TextProject.org to be easy to implement and engaging for his students. The Word Pictures depict vocabulary within some of the clusters outlined in Table 3.2. An example of a semantic map is provided in Figure 3.2, for one of the

Figure 3.2. Example of a Semantic Map in TextProject's Word Pictures

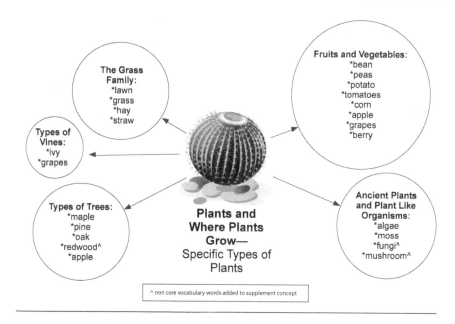

The Grass Family:
*lawn
*grass
*hay
*straw

Fruits and Vegetables:
*bean
*peas
*potato
*tomatoes
*corn
*apple
*grapes
*berry

Types of Vines:
*ivy
*grapes

Types of Trees:
*maple
*pine
*oak
*redwood^
*apple

Plants and Where Plants Grow— Specific Types of Plants

Ancient Plants and Plant Like Organisms:
*algae
*moss
*fungi^
*mushroom^

^ non core vocabulary words added to supplement concept

categories within the cluster on Plants and Where Plants Grow, a topic of study in Joshua's classroom. He uses the semantic map in Figure 3.2 as the basis for a word wall and adds available pictures for more unusual words (e.g., *fungi, algae, ivy*). Over the course of a 2-week period, students add words to categories. For example, after Joshua read aloud *Wangari's Trees of Peace* (Winter, 2008), students became interested in trees indigenous to Africa. Their research led to the addition of baobab and fig to types of trees on the semantic map and helped students to enjoy taking charge of additional learning.

Core Reading

Joshua knows how important it is to keep track of students' recognition of core vocabulary words. After all, this vocabulary is the foundation of students' ability to read with comprehension and confidence. He has found that the Reading GPS system available at TextProject. org is a useful free tool for capturing his students' progress on the core vocabulary. The examples in Table 3.3 illustrate how the texts in this assessment have been written to correlate with the vocabulary of instructional texts (see Table 3.1).

This correlation allows Joshua to use information from the assessment to select texts for small-group instruction and follow-up learning center activities. Joshua uses a variety of programs in his classroom, but when he wants to give his students concen-

> *The Reading GPS system available at TextProject.org is a useful free tool for capturing his students' progress on the core vocabulary.*

trated experiences with the core vocabulary, he knows that programs such as *BeginningReads* and *FYI for Kids* (TextProject.org) will accomplish that goal, because the texts in these programs have been written to emphasize the words in specific word zones.

Choice Reading

Joshua has observed that some students have a hard time knowing what to read during choice reading. To support students in developing strong independent reading habits, Joshua makes available texts that are associated with the topic of the collection of words. During the unit on Plants and Where Plants Grow, for example, he ensures that a group of trade books on plants is prominent in the classroom's book center. Among trade books on the topic of plants that have proven to be favorites of Joshua's students are:

- *A Tree Is Nice* (Udry, 1987)
- *A Tree Is a Plant* (Bulla, 2016)
- *A Weed Is a Flower: The Life of George Washington Carver* (Aliki, 1988)
- *The Dandelion Seed* (Anthony, 1997)
- *Tell Me, Tree: All About Trees for Kids* (Gibbons, 2002)
- *We Planted a Tree* (Muldrow, 2016)

THE LAST WORD

Beginning reading texts changed substantially in the early 1990s when large states such as California and Texas demanded that their programs have only authentic texts, which were defined as texts from the trade divisions of publishers and not ones written specifically for educational use. The number of new words per 100 words in end-of-year, 1st-grade texts doubled from 10 in the mid-1980s to

Table 3.3. Assessments to Capture Core Vocabulary Proficiency

Level	Text Example (1st paragraph)[1]	Target Core Vocabulary	Open-Access Follow-up Text[2]
Level A	**Skunks keep** themselves safe **by giving off a bad smell. The smell tells people and other animals to go away.**	Word zones 1 and 2 and words with short vowels (e.g., *bad*)	BeginningReads, stages 1–5
Level B	**Tree frogs are animals that live in trees and grasses around water. Tree frogs blend in with things around them.**	Word zones 1 and 2 and words with short vowels (e.g., *frog*) and long vowels (e.g., *tree*)	BeginningReads, stages 6–10
Level C	**Bee flies are insects that act and look just like bees. Bees go from** flower **to** flower, **drinking** nectar. **Bee flies also go from** flower **to** flower, **drinking** nectar.	Word zones 1 to 3 and words with short vowels (e.g., *drinking*) and long vowels (e.g., *bees*)	• FYI for Kids, Level 1 • SummerReads, Grade 3

1. The words in bold in the text examples are ones that are part of the target core vocabulary.
2. These texts and others are available for free download at TextProject.org.

20 in the early 1990s (Hiebert, 2005b). This pattern of a high number of new words per 100 words is still evident in the 1st-grade texts of current core reading programs and leveled texts. High numbers of new words per 100 words mean that few of the new words are repeated. The need to recognize numerous new words in one text, then another set of new words in the next text, and so on, requires considerable effort on the part of beginning and struggling readers. When confronted with so many new words from text to text, some students can have a hard time becoming facile with the core vocabulary.

I am not advocating a return to the controlled text of the Dick-and-Jane era, where text was stilted and bland. But alternatives exist, one of which is a genre that I call intentional texts. In intentional texts, the majority of words come from specific bands of core vocabulary. Rare words are included in these texts but they are always repeated at least several times. These intentionally written texts can be engaging and informative, as illustrated by the texts from the Reading GPS system in Table 3.3. Even in a text that relies on the 300 most frequent words (e.g., *Skunks* in Table 3.3), engaging information can be conveyed.

Texts with intentional design should be part of the text diet of beginning and struggling readers. Text diets should be rich and inclusive, including texts written by well-known children's authors as well as engaging and informative texts that have been created intentionally to emphasize the words and knowledge that form the foundation for proficient and lifelong reading.

CHAPTER 4

A Short History of English and Why It Matters

Example 1: Goldlöckchen sahen ein Haus. Sie klopfte an die Tür. Niemand antwortete. Sie ging hinein.

Example 2: Boucle d'or a vu une maison. Elle a frappé à la porte. Personne n'a répondu. Elle est entrée.

The words in these two text excerpts will look vaguely familiar to you as a proficient reader of English. In the first example in German, you might guess several meanings: *sahen* (saw), *Haus* (house), and *ging* (going or went). In the French version, you likely will recognize a number of words that resemble English words: *personne* (person), *répondu* (respond), *entrée* (entered), *maison* (mansion), and *vu* (view). All of the English words cannot be figured out from the German and French examples, but, for most readers of English, the gist is likely clear, especially since the story is well-known: *Goldilocks saw a house. She knocked on the door. No one answered. She went in.*

English has strong connections to both German and French. Together, they are responsible for the majority of English words. These two systems are important to understand because each has a different morphological system—and morphological awareness is critical in being facile with the word families in the core vocabulary. A third language also contributes to English—Greek. The Greek contributions to English are fewer in number than those of German and French but the Greek morphological system is critical for understanding many technical words.

THE EVIDENCE

English has words from many languages, including but not limited to Arabic, Japanese, Chinese, and American indigenous languages, but the majority of words in English—and the ways in which root words are changed to generate new meanings—emanate from the three systems of Anglo-Saxon (German origins), French (Latin origins), and Greek. A short history of English helps to clarify the morphological systems of English.

Anglo-Saxon Foundation

Many of the commonly used words in English today have roots in the language of the Anglo-Saxons. The Anglos and the Saxons were Germanic groups who invaded and conquered England in the 5th and 6th centuries. The origins of English typically are described as Anglo-Saxon, but since the language of the Anglos and Saxons was based in German, this layer of English has many similarities to the German language. For that reason, the language used in the introductory example of this chapter was German.

To understand the content of the Anglo-Saxon words in English, think of what life was like in the 5th and 6th centuries. Most people lived in the countryside, farming the land. Many also were involved with the sea that surrounded much of England, as fishermen, ship builders, and sailors. Words in Table 4.1 illustrate the kinds of content words in English that are from Anglo-Saxon—words related to water, land, and the home. Many verbs also stem from Anglo-Saxon words, such as *sit/sitzen, speak/sprechen,* and *eat/essen,* as do prepositions, including *and/und, over/über,* and *in/im.*

Root words in the Anglo-Saxon layer of English are often monosyllabic, as is evident in the first two columns in Table 4.1, where all but two of the 35 words—*water, weather*—are monosyllabic. Plurals (e.g., *pigs, ducks*) and possessives (*pig's, duck's*) are added to nouns in fairly consistent ways, as are inflected endings to verbs (e.g., *snows, snowing, snowed*).

The prefixes and suffixes added to Anglo-Saxon words are few, especially in comparison to English words of French origin. Among the most prominent Anglo-Saxon prefixes are a- (e.g., *asleep, awake*), over- (e.g., *overjoyed, overflow*), and mis- (e.g., *misspell, misfire*). Typical of Anglo-Saxon suffixes are -less (e.g., *helpless, careless*), -ful (e.g.,

Table 4.1. Examples of Types of Anglo-Saxon Words

Category	Category Members	Compound Words Related to Category
barn	duck, hen, cow, pig, sheep	barnyard, duckbill, henpeck, cowboy, pigpen, sheepskin
food	bread, crop, grow, meat, seed, land	foodstuff, breadbox, croplands, grownup, meatball, seedeater, landfill
house	bed, room, clean, broom	housebound, bedcover, roommate, cleanup, broomstick
woods	tree, chop, cut, fox, snake, hare	woodland, treetop, chopstick, cutback, foxhunt, snakebite, harebrained
sea	ship, sail, water, swim	seafloor, shipworm, sailboat, waterwheel, swimsuit
weather	snow, rain, wet, sun	weathercast, snowfall, raincoat, wetland, sunrise

cupful, painful), and -ish (e.g., *childish, selfish*). As these examples illustrate, the meanings of Anglo-Saxon affixes are relatively straightforward.

The addition of plurals, possessives, and inflected endings occurs across other language groups in English, but the distinguishing feature of the Anglo-Saxon layer of English is the creation of new words by combining two or more existing words to make compound words. The number of compound words associated with the content words in the first two columns of Table 4.1 is far greater than the examples given in the third column. In addition to the example for *house* in Table 4.1—*housebound*—the *Oxford English Dictionary* (Stevenson, 2015) lists 50 other words where *house* is the first or descriptor word in a compound (e.g., *housesitter, housewarming*) and 83 words where house is the second or base word in a compound (e.g., *greenhouse, doghouse*).

Creating new words by combining words is not just a phenomenon of the past. Compound words are a primary source for the labels of new inventions or experiences (Baugh & Cable, 2012). When personal computers began to appear in the early 1980s, a whole vocabulary quickly was created. Many of these words combined existing words from the Anglo-Saxon layer of English, as is evident in *laptop, software, mousepad,* and *keyboard.* Most parts of speech can be used in compound words, but the most typical compound words involve a noun as the base or second word and a word added in front that describes the noun. The descriptors added to the noun can be another noun (e.g., *football*), an adjective (e.g., *blackboard*), or a verb (e.g., *breakwater*).

> One of the challenges of compound words is that there are no hard-and-fast rules about the meanings of compound words.

For students learning to read, one of the challenges of compound words is that there are no hard-and-fast rules about the meanings of compound words. Sometimes the meanings are obvious, but in other cases they need to be inferred. A throwaway is something that is to be discarded, but a throwback is not something that physically is thrown behind someone's back. Neither does anything necessarily get thrown through the air in a government overthrow. In geology, a downthrow involves the sinking of rocks on one side of a faulty plane, not a physical projectile moving through the air.

The making of compound words is one of the contributions of the Anglo-Saxon part of English. The root words in this layer of English may pertain to fairly common concepts, but compound words with meanings that can be idiosyncratic can add a level of complexity to English, especially for students who speak a native language other than English.

The French Connection

In 1066, the Normans, who spoke a form of French, invaded and conquered England. The power of the conquering group meant that French became the language of the kings and high culture, including the law, arts, and clergy. The French words in the Goldilocks excerpt in the introduction of the chapter illustrate the kind of words that entered into English from French. These words were typically synonyms for existing words in the Anglo-Saxon layer of English, as can be seen in Table 4.2. These synonyms, such as cuisine for food, were almost always multisyllabic.

Because the aristocracy and upper classes used French, the French words were associated with more sophisticated ways of expression than the Anglo-Saxon words (Crystal, 2010). For example, *sovereign* was the word used for *king* and *felony* for *crime*.

The upper classes spoke French but the people who worked the farms, manned the ships, and chopped trees in the woods continued

Table 4.2. Words in English with Anglo-Saxon and French Roots

Anglo-Saxon	French
food	cuisine, nourishment
church	sanctuary
weather	climate
sea	ocean
woods	forest
house	residence
barn	grange
clothes	garments, fashion

to speak Anglo-Saxon. Then political tides changed and, by the late 14th century, the English court was speaking Anglo-Saxon instead of French (Barber, Beal, & Shaw, 2009). However, the trace of French vocabulary remained. English was no longer the German-based, Anglo-Saxon language but a hybrid with numerous French-based words. In particular, writers tended to use the French-based words to show themselves to be scholarly and well-educated. Writing tends to be more formal than the oral language of conversations, and so French-based words continue to be more prominent in written language than in oral language (Biber & Conrad, 2016). Many words in literary or academic texts have their origins in French.

French is one of the languages (the others are Spanish, Italian, Portuguese, and Romanian) that originated in Latin and are referred to as Romance languages. In Romance languages, a single root word is the source of numerous related words. Consider, for example, the root word *rupt*, which means "to break." With prefixes and suffixes, this root word is at the center of an extensive family of words, as shown in Figure 4.1. Inflected endings have not been included in Figure 4.1, but they operate similarly to the Anglo-Saxon layer of English: The endings -ed, -ing, and -s are added to show changes in tense (e.g., *interrupted, interrupting, interrupts*) or in number (e.g., *interruptions*).

In many cases, the root words and the affixes used in Romance languages are quite similar to the French-origin words in English. For the numerous Spanish speakers in the United States, many words that are used in conversational Spanish are connected closely to the French-origin literary and academic vocabulary of English. These

Figure 4.1. English Words Derived from Root *rupt*

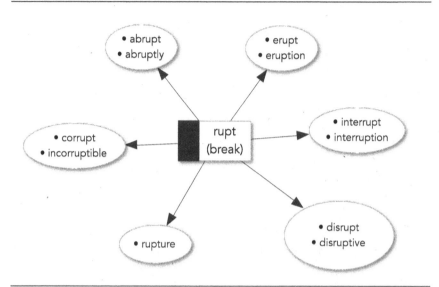

words, called cognates, can be a valuable resource for native Spanish speakers in comprehending school texts, as will be described in more depth in Chapter 9 ("Different Labels but the Same Concepts: English Learners").

Scientific and Technical Words from Greek

The scientific revolution that began in the 16th century resulted in new inventions and technologies. Think about the invention of the telescope. Initially, the device was given the name *Dutch perspective glasses*, but it generated attention when Galileo increased the magnification and pointed the instrument to the sky. At that point, the instrument was given the name *telescope*—from the Greek roots *tele* (far) and *skopos* (to observe).

As this example shows, scientists and inventors of the Renaissance turned to Greek and Latin to provide names that they considered credible (Baugh & Cable, 2012). Many Latin words used to describe scientific terms had been derived from Greek, but during the scientific revolution, scientists and inventors also went to the original Greek to label processes and phenomena.

When original Greek words were used for naming processes and phenomena, yet another way of generating new words was added to English. Typically, Greek roots combine in compound words where both of the constituents have "equal" weight, as in the following examples:

> *arachno* (spider) + *phobia* (fear of) as in *arachnophobia*: the fear of spiders
>
> *micro* (small) + *scope* (instrument for viewing) as in *microscope*: instrument for viewing small things
>
> *demos* (people) + *cracy* (power, rule) as in *democracy*: government by the people

Some Greek roots, such as *phobia*, can function on their own, but Greek roots often are combined to name new processes and phenomena (e.g., *chemotherapy, geometric*).

A Cacophony of Languages and Inventions

The vast majority of the words in English come from the three sources that have just been described. But English speakers use words from many additional languages daily, often without knowing the languages from which words originate. Further, as new ideas and inventions arise, existing words take on new meanings and new words are coined.

Geographic exploration adds new words to English. The scientific discoveries of the Renaissance also contributed to better ways of building ships and navigation. The improved forms of transportation led to trade between England and other countries in Europe, the Middle East, and Asia. This trade brought new words into English, including words from the Arabic language such as *peach* and *apricot*. But, more important, Arabic words for concepts related to mathematics entered into English and changed the counting system (e.g., *zero*) and mathematics (e.g., *algebra, algorithms*).

Beginning in the late 16th century, England became a primary participant in the colonization of lands new to the European countries. When explorers encountered new phenomena, they needed labels to identify what they found. Sometimes, explorers adopted the labels of the indigenous people but, inevitably, the words of the indigenous people were changed to the sounds and spellings of the explorers' language. When the English explorers encountered new animals in North America, for example, words from indigenous languages were transformed into English forms. Examples of the roots of English words in various Algonquian dialects include *raccoon* (*aroughcun*), *skunk* (*seganku*), and *moose* (*moos*). Other times, the English explorers combined existing English words to describe phenomena new to them (Hogg & Denison, 2006). Evidence of the use of compounding of English words to label flora and fauna unique to North America include *redwood, gooseberry*, and *western gull*.

As colonies gained independence from Britain, distinctive forms of vocabulary began to be added to English. Canadians, New Zealanders, Australians, Indians, Pakistanis, and South Africans all added words to English (Bryson, 2001). The United States, with its vast population, has been a primary source for many additions to the dictionary and many new meanings for existing words (Bryson, 2015). These differences were evident in the release of the *Harry Potter* series. First published in Great Britain, the release of individual titles of the series was delayed in the United States to permit translations of vocabulary words. For example, in the American edition, *cookies* replaced *biscuits*, *trunk* replaced *boot*, and *apartment* replaced *flat*.

Inventions add new words to English. Scientific advancements have meant that inventions have flourished. Each new invention requires new labels for processes and objects. Words from the film industry, as shown in Table 4.3, illustrate the ways in which new words and new meanings for existing words are added to English. Compounding is one way of creating new words, as illustrated by *close-up* in Table 4.3. Other words such as *cinematography* reflect the use of Greek roots to add credibility and sophistication to a field. The word *technicolor* illustrates how Greek roots (*techno*) are combined with French ones (*color*).

When the new industry of the movies had similar components to the theater, such as scripts and actors, the meanings of these words were extended. In other cases, new meanings were given to words that had no apparent connection to play-acting. Such is the case with *trailer*, which centuries ago referred to a hound or huntsman who followed a trail. Sometime later, the word was used to describe a vehicle pulled by another. This meaning of a trailer continues, but in the movie industry, trailer has come to refer to a preview of a coming movie.

Table 4.3. Origins of Words Associated with a New Invention

Word	Source
cinematography	compound of *cinema* from Greek (movement) + *graphy* (process of writing or recording)
close-up	compound of two common Anglo-Saxon words
lines	existing from a related industry (theater)
pan	existing Anglo-Saxon word but giving it a new meaning (moving a camera across a screen)
script	existing word from a related industry (theater)
technicolor	compound of *techno-* (art, skill, craft) from Greek + *color* from French/Latin
thriller	existing Anglo-Saxon word with the addition of a suffix to create a new word (or meaning)
trailer	existing Anglo-Saxon word but used in a unique manner

SMALL CHANGES = BIG RESULTS

Mariana is a 5th-grade teacher who has made several small changes in her English/Language Arts instruction. The focal point of these changes has been morphological content because Mariana knows how essential this knowledge is in 5th-grade content and in the middle-school curriculum that her students will be encountering soon.

Conversations

A consistent strategy among students in Mariana's 5th-grade classroom is to ask, when encountering a new word, "Do I know the root word?" To make use of this capacity, however, students need to be cognizant of root words and how families of words are created in the three layers of English. In conversations, Mariana makes frequent use of the vocabulary triangle (Calfee & Drum, 1986) in Figure 4.2, which is prominently displayed in her classroom.

The placement of the three linguistic sources in the vocabulary triangle gives an indication of the contributions of the words from each language to English. Anglo-Saxon words form the base of the triangle, accounting for the foundational words in English. The French-origin words "add on" or build on the Anglo-Saxon words, while the

Figure 4.2. Vocabulary Triangle Illustrating Sources of English Vocabulary

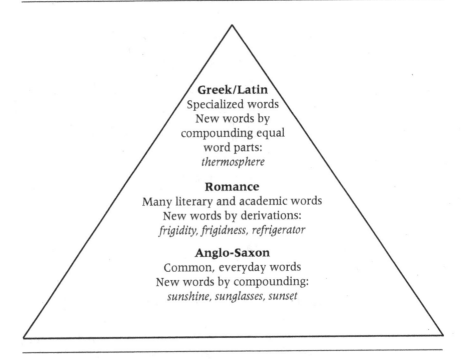

Greek- and Latin-origin words are fewest in number but have a critical role in content-area topics.

Core Reading

The layer of the word triangle that Mariana especially emphasizes as she prepares her students for middle school is the French layer of English. Word families with French roots can be expected to become increasingly more apparent in the content-area texts of middle school. The French-based word families add new words in fairly predictable ways. To demonstrate these patterns, Mariana has selected a small group of word families to illustrate how different suffixes and prefixes change meanings or functions in word families (see Table 4.4). Mariana knows that students do not need to be taught the patterns of every single morphological family from the French layer of English. She has chosen to identify this handful of families to aid her students in developing the morphological awareness that allows them to generalize to other words and their families.

Table 4.4. Five Target French-Based Morphological Families for Demonstrating Effects on Meaning of Suffixes and Prefixes*

Root Word	Suffixes	Prefixes
character	characteristic/characteristically characterize/characterization characterless	uncharacteristic/ uncharacteristically
acquire	acquisitive/acquisitiveness acquisition acquisitor acquirement	unacquisitive reacquire
associate (adjective & noun: /əˈsōshēət/) (verb: əˈsōsēˌāt)	association associative associable	disassociate
precise	precision precisely preciseness	imprecise imprecision overprecise
significant	signify significance significantly	insignificance nonsignificant

*This list represents a sampling of the members of word families and is not comprehensive.

Similarity in meaning for some suffixes can be deduced with good examples such as those in Table 4.4. For instance, when presenting sets of words such as *precise/precision, acquire/acquisition,* and *associate/ association,* Mariana asks her students to hypothesize how the meanings of the root words change when the suffix is added. For other suffixes, such as the -ize in *characterize,* the discussion is more extended. For this discussion, she includes the words *apologize* and *crystallize* because she knows that the suffix -ize can influence root words differently. In the case of *characterize,* the uniqueness or distinctive character of something/one is being identified or described. In *crystallize* and *apologize,* something is being made—a *crystal* or an *apology.*

The nuances that can occur in the meanings created by the addition of suffixes illustrate the advantage of the instructional approach that Mariana is taking: Focus is on the changes in meaning wrought by adding the prefixes and suffixes to root words, not on memorizing the meanings of individual prefixes and suffixes. On their own, the prefixes and suffixes are hard to nail down.

Collections of Words

Mariana uses the five focus families in Table 4.4 as the basis for a word collection. The task for students is to identify words from other families that use similar affixes. The list of words with -ion is massive, including words that are used frequently in the classroom, such as *communication, comprehension,* and *investigation.*

Based on the use of the words in texts that they are reading, students attach summaries of the effect of the affix on the root. One student's conclusion was: "When you add -ion to a verb such as *associate* or *acquire,* you're showing the result of the action. Acquisition is the result of acquiring; association is the result of associating."

At another time of the year, Mariana has students determine whether words take on different meanings in different content areas. For example, in chemistry, association refers to the linking of molecules. Students also have noted how frequently *association* is used in proper names such as National Basketball Association and in acronyms where association is one of the constituents, as in FIFA (Fédération Internationale de Football Association).

Choice Reading

In the phrase *choice reading, choice* signals that the intention of the activity is for students to select their own texts for reading, but Mariana knows that *choice* is not a synonym for *anything goes.* A lifelong habit of independent reading is built on knowing about different genres, authors, and topics of texts. The foundation of such knowledge comes from conversations and modeling by teachers and peers.

In tune with the content of this chapter—that knowledge about the history of English can support readers' development of vocabulary—some of the book talks in Mariana's classroom revolve around books on the origins of different words in English. Mariana has found that a set of free downloadable texts on word origins at TextProject.org—a series called *Stories of Words*—can support students in learning about the origins of words. The 16 texts in the *Stories of Words* series fall into four categories: (1) contributions from other languages (e.g., Spanish, Arabic), (2) language structures (e.g., toponyms, abbreviations), (3) inventions (e.g., computers, movies), and (4) themes (e.g., music, clothes). Mariana has found that the *Stories of Words* series has motivated her students to study the origin of words.

> *Getting students excited about word origins does not have to be tedious.*

One student who had emigrated from India noticed the lack of any reference to English words with Hindi origins in the *Stories of Words* series. This student began to collect a group of words and, much to the delight of her peers, found that the word *avatar* comes from Hindi. As her list kept growing to include *punch*, *shampoo*, and *pajamas*, the interest of the class grew, and others began to pursue similar projects on words related to topics of interest.

THE LAST WORD

English is a complex language that reflects its history. Some awareness about the origins of English can go a long way to developing the foundation for proficient reading. The word some is emphasized, because the goal is awareness of morphological forms and their influence, rather than the recitation of facts about the historical roots of English. Getting students excited about word origins does not have to be tedious. The actions of the 4Cs can support students in using their morphological awareness to establish the meanings of previously unknown words as they read. Recognition of how different systems in English work is a valuable resource in using texts to gain the knowledge about the social and physical world that is so essential to life in the 21st century. In addition, in today's multicultural classrooms, the multilingual origins of English can be a source of pride for students and can make newcomers feel more at home.

CHAPTER 5

Recycling and Remixing
Multiple Meanings and Uses of Words

> *Example 1:* My problems started when I learned that Mrs. Reno would be my fourth grade teacher. She had a lizard in her classroom, and lizards were on my list of terrifying things. (*Lizard Problems*, Adams, 2009)

> *Example 2:* Wilbur looked at his friend. She looked rather swollen and she seemed listless. "I'm awfully sorry to hear that you're feeling poorly, Charlotte," he said. "Perhaps if you spin a web and catch a couple of flies you'll feel better." (*Charlotte's Web*, White, 1952, Chapter 8)

For good readers, reading is an active process. No, they're not throwing a basketball into a hoop or jumping up and down as they might during a sporting event, but active readers are thinking continuously about what they are reading. Amy (the narrator in *Lizard Problems*) may have an unusual list—things of which she's terrified—but most students will be familiar with the concept of a *list* as "a number of connected items presented consecutively, typically one below the other" (dictionary.com) when they encounter that word in Example 1. The meaning of the word *list* as a tabulation dominates in student texts, making the word *listless* in Example 2 potentially confusing. Active readers who do not understand the meaning of this word will review the previous paragraph, where Charlotte described herself as tired and not having energy. Further, Wilbur's description that Charlotte is "feeling poorly" leads to the conclusion that listless must have something to do with low energy and nothing at all to do with Charlotte's lack of a list similar to Amy's in Example 1.

Active readers monitor their understanding as they read, revisiting parts of text to clarify meaning. Monitoring is built on the capacity to be flexible as a reader. Flexible readers approach texts with the expectation that words can take on different meanings in different contexts. Flexibility when encountering familiar and unfamiliar words is especially critical with the words in the core vocabulary. The lead words that represent the 2,500 morphological families have, on average, seven

> *Flexible readers approach texts with the expectation that words can take on different meanings in different contexts.*

different meanings, according to WordNet (Miller, 1995). Some of these meanings are subtle; others are dramatic, reflecting different origins of a word with the same pronunciation. There are two fundamental ways in which the meanings of words change: processes called recycling and remixing in this book. Recycling is when the same word can take on different meanings. Remixing is the combining of words.

Contemporary students understand the concept of objects being reused or recycled. Just like objects can be reused, words also get reused or recycled. The word *list* illustrates the process of recycling. In the Anglo-Saxon era, English had a word *list* that meant "to be pleased, desire." Several centuries later a French word, *liste*, which meant "band, row, group," came into English vocabulary. As this new meaning of list became prominent, the use of list to refer to pleasure or enjoyment became obsolete. However, the adjective *listless*—meaning to be without pleasure or enjoyment—remained. Giving new meanings to existing words is a process that occurred not only far in the past. Recycling of word meanings is rampant in the age of the Internet. For example, a *footprint* can now refer to the amount of carbon compounds from fossil fuel consumption left on Earth from the actions of a person or group, not simply a track or mark left by a foot or shoe.

Students also may know about remixing—where songs are mixed together to create a unique song. At the very least, students will know about mixing ingredients, as when eggs and milk are combined to make French toast or when eggs, peanut butter, and sugar result in tasty cookies. Remixing of words, similarly, involves combining words in compound words or phrases to convey a new meaning. For example, new words that were added to dictionaries in 2019 include *bingeable* (having multiple episodes or parts of a show that can be watched in rapid succession) and *permalink* (permanent static hyperlink). Words also are combined in new ways to create expressions such as *to table*, which refers to postponing a discussion or event.

THE EVIDENCE

Both recycling and remixing have a number of forms that can be useful for teachers to keep in mind when creating lessons and holding discussions.

How Words Get Different Meanings: Recycling

The meanings of a word can shift with a change in the part of speech. The meanings associated with words also can change, sometimes gradually and other times quickly. Homonyms are another example of different meanings associated with the same word form. The use of some words and word meanings also can diminish over time, dropping out of contemporary use.

Parts of speech change, word meanings change. The meanings of many words vary when the words are used as different parts of speech, even without the addition of endings. The word *lap* has distinctive meanings in the following sentences, which come from decodable texts for beginning readers:

The cat sat in Pam's lap.
Cats lap up milk.
The waves lap onto the rocks.

The meaning of *lap* as a noun and a verb varies considerably. Young children likely understand the idea of a cat or child sitting in someone's lap, but the use of the word *lap* to refer to drinking with quick movements or the actions of waves may not be familiar to some young children.

Nouns also can become verbs by adding -ing, as when *rain* becomes *raining*. Often, the use of a noun as a verb happens first in conversations and popular media, such as *emailing, texting, messaging,* and *blogging.* Saying, "I'm blogging," is shorter and snappier than saying, "I am writing a blog." Over time, the use of a noun as a verb becomes an accepted form.

Another way words change is when verbs become nouns. For example, *adapt* becomes *adaptation* or *reveal* becomes *revelation.* The process of changing a verb into a noun removes the action, making already-abstract words even more abstract. Further, the addition of syllables as a verb becomes a noun can make pronunciation challenging for some students, while shifts in spelling (e.g., *reveal/revelation*) can make it difficult for students to link the meanings of the words.

Word meanings morph. The word *morph* in this subheading illustrates the ways in which meanings of words change. Originally, *meta* (change) and *morpheus* (shape, form) were combined to form *metamorphosis*, meaning a transformation. This word moved from use in biology (insects or amphibians moving from an immature to adult form) to use in computer animation. Now the word have been shortened to *morph* and is used in a variety of contexts, such as when a person or thing (including word meanings) changes.

Unless meanings of a word have different historical origins, connections across different meanings of the same word usually can be understood with a quick study. That is certainly the case with many of the words that have been given new meanings in the digital era. The word *viral*, which describes information circulated rapidly on the Internet, connects to *virus*, an infection that spreads rapidly. Or *tweet*, which refers to a short post on a social media site, connects to its original meaning of tweet, a short (and often repeated) sound of a bird.

Homonyms. Homonym is a label for words that have the same spelling and sound but have different meanings (e.g., *duck* as a noun—a waterbird; *duck* as a verb—lower the head). The reason for these different meanings reflect unique histories of concepts that came to be pronounced and spelled exactly the same.

Homonyms frequently get lumped together with homographs (words with similar spellings but different pronunciations) and homophones (words that sound the same but have different spellings and meanings) in the elementary English/Language Arts curriculum. But homonyms are distinctive from these other two groups of words, especially when the focus of instruction is on supporting students with the multiple meanings of words. Homonyms, unlike the other two groups of words, are sets of words with the same pronunciation and spelling but with quite distinctive meanings. The words that fall into this category are frequent and distinctive in meaning—words such as *back, bark, can, seal, trip,* and *well.*

Often, a focus of elementary instruction is on homophones (e.g., *their, there, they're*) but, while these words sound the same, their unique spellings in written language mean that readers have a clue to their meaning. When words such as *club, can,* and *bear* appear in text, however, their meanings can be confusing for readers. Unlike homophones, which often are the focus of instruction, homonyms merit attention because of their unique meanings.

Archaic words. The discussion of recycling of word meanings is not complete without addressing words in the dictionary landfill—words that dictionary writers describe as archaic and that are no longer used in conversations and texts. Words such as cackle, hayfield, and fib were among the known and important words for middle graders in the Dale–Chall (1948) readability formula. These words may have been prominent in the late 1940s when Dale and Chall identified the words for their list, but contemporary students typically do not hear or use these words.

A problem with archaic words can be their presence on summative assessments because of test-makers' use of public domain texts that are royalty-free. These public domain texts, all published in 1923 or earlier, are rife with archaic language. To become proficient at reading such texts requires an awareness of the language used in older texts and some experience with them. It's impossible to introduce students to all possible variations of texts with archaic language, but even a handful of examples can support students' awareness and expectations of language in texts from bygone eras. The following excerpts from Kipling's *The Jungle Book* and from Lofting's *The Story of Doctor Dolittle* illustrate the vocabulary of older texts (e.g., *thou, hast, ye, lest, pshaw*).

> "Out!" snapped Father Wolf. ". . . Thou hast done harm enough for one night."
> "I go," said Tabaqui quietly. "Ye can hear Shere Khan below in the thickets. I might have saved myself the message." (Kipling, 1894)
> "He has taken care not to blubber or sniffle, lest we should find out that he is crying. . . . Pshaw!—Such ignorance!" sniffed Too-Too. (Lofting, 1920)

Remixing Meanings

When words are mixed together, the resulting word or phrase does not necessarily retain the precise meanings of the individual words. Phrases where words are remixed are of three types: (1) complex phrases, which are prominent in content areas, (2) figurative language, including idioms, and (3) collocations, words commonly used together.

Complex phrases. Linguists may define *climate change, water cycle,* or *House of Representatives* as open compound words, meaning that they are neither hyphenated nor combined but convey a unique meaning as a set of words. Open compound words in everyday contexts, such as in the phrases *water cooler* or *cold water*, are fairly straightforward in their meaning (although a picture may be useful for water cooler for some students). In content areas, however, open compounds such as *water cycle* and *water table* are quite precise and involve concepts that go considerably beyond the typical words in a compound word. For example, *water cycle* means more than *water* (a liquid) and *cycle* (a series of events); it refers to the circulation of water on Earth, involving an extended series of events that include precipitation, evaporation, condensation, and transpiration.

Because of the complexity of many compound words in content areas, I have suggested that compound words in content areas are better treated as complex phrases than simply as compound words (Hiebert & Bravo, 2010). Examples of compound words that function as complex phrases in content areas are given in Table 5.1 to demonstrate why many compound words in content areas deserve treatment as complex phrases.

Figurative language. In figurative language, the meanings of the words that have been remixed are neither precise (as in complex phrases) nor literal. Poetry provides the quintessential examples of figurative language. A stanza from Emily Dickinson's poem "The Railway Train" (1891) illustrates the way in which words are mixed together to create images.

> I like to see it lap the miles,
> And lick the valleys up,
> And stop to feed itself at tanks;
> And then, prodigious, step . . .

Every word in this poem except for *prodigious* is in the core vocabulary. But verbs such as *lap, lick, feed,* and *step* require the reader to imagine an inanimate object taking on actions associated with humans or animals.

Table 5.1. Examples of Compound Words That Function as Complex Phrases in Content Areas (4th Grade)

Content Area	Examples of Complex Phrase	Meaning
Mathematics	• Place value • Proper fraction	• Value represented by a digit in a number on the basis of its position in the number • A fraction whose numerator is less than the denominator
Social Studies	• Capital resources • Human resources	• Goods made by people and used to produce other goods and services • People who do physical or mental work to produce goods or services
Science	• Change of state • Food chain	• A physical change that occurs when matter changes to another state (i.e., liquid, gas, or solid) • Transfer of energy through various stages as a result of feeding patterns of a series of organisms

Narrative texts are usually not as dense with figurative language as poetry. But some authors use figurative language frequently. Further, some picture books are a visual expression of figurative language. Such is the case with *Quick as a Cricket* (Wood, 1982), where a young child's capabilities are presented as similes (*loud as a lion, tough as a rhino,* etc.). Students can enjoy listening to the examples from Wood's book and then creating and sharing their own. These student inventions can be the focus of a collection of words—one of the 4Cs of small changes.

Idioms. Idioms are a form of figurative language that often is used in conversations but that also can appear in dialogue in narrative texts and, in some cases, may be the source of a picture book. Idioms have meanings that cannot be established by the literal definitions of the individual words in a phrase. For example, the expression *it cost an arm and a leg* is not meant to be interpreted literally. Because idioms occur as part of informal or casual communication of conversations, words in idioms are usually from the core vocabulary. Consequently, these words will be counted as easy in current text complexity schemes, but that does not make these expressions easy for young readers or non-native English speakers. Teachers who are native English speakers need to be aware that the meanings of idioms that they take for granted may not be evident to all students.

> *Because idioms occur as part of informal or casual communication of conversations, words in idioms are usually from the core vocabulary. Consequently, these words will be counted as easy in current text complexity schemes, but that does not make these expressions easy for young readers or non-native English speakers.*

Another way teachers can support their non-native English speakers is to highlight the universality of idioms. All languages have idioms but rarely are the same idioms used across languages. For example, English idioms for being in good health are *fit as a fiddle* or *healthy as a horse,* while a Spanish equivalent is *estar más sano que una pera,* or, literally, to be healthier than a pear. The explanation behind this expression—that pears are viewed to have high nutritional value—shows that most idioms (including English ones) depend on shared knowledge within a culture.

Collocations. As teachers work with students on using context to make meaning of words and text, knowing about collocations can be useful. The term *collocation* refers to words that often occur together. The word *chocolate* often is followed by *bar, cake,* or *chip.* If *chocolate* appears in a phrase with *cookie,* the likely word to follow *chocolate* is *chip.* Collocations differ from complex phrases because the words in the group are not fixed but will vary, depending on the context. Another difference is that the collocations formed by two or three words do not have a formal definition, in contrast to complex phrases, such as *climate change* or *water cycle.* Developing ease with collocations such as *freezing cold* or *bitter cold,* however, can be highly supportive in reading smoothly and meaningfully.

The number of collocations in language is far too large for comprehensive coverage (Nesselhauf, 2005). Unlike instruction on complex phrases, where students need to associate a group of words as having a specific meaning, instruction on collocations encourages students to use the context of sentences to anticipate and predict what is likely to come before *cold* or after *chocolate.*

SMALL CHANGES = BIG RESULTS

Instruction about recycling and remixing words is essential in every grade and every subject area, but this facet of word knowledge becomes increasingly vital as students move to the upper elementary grades, where texts are longer and have more complicated themes. A visit to the 4th-grade classroom of Francine illustrates small changes related to word recycling and remixing that can be integrated into daily teaching routines.

Core Reading

Francine conducts a mini-lesson about multiple-meaning words early in the school year as part of her core reading instruction. She creates a semantic map of a word that she knows will arise across the school year in her classroom: *craft*. (See Figure 5.1.)

Francine chose this word because the term *author's craft* is prominent in her state's English/Language Arts standards and therefore is likely to appear on the end-of-the-year assessment. She also knows that *craft* shows up in many children's books, as in *Exploring the Titanic* (Ballard, 1988), where *craft* is used to describe a boat, and that a derivative of this word—*crafty*—appears in *James and the Giant Peach* (Dahl, 1961) in quite a unique way to mean sly, tricky, or devious.

Conversations

At the end of the first mini-lesson on multiple-meaning words, Francine and her students discuss how best to summarize what they have learned. Francine adds a word reminder to a chart she displays prominently in her classroom. Over the course of the school year, more word reminders are added to the chart as more word patterns are studied. Figure 5.2 shows such a chart.

In addition to the classroom chart, Francine has given her students 3 x 5 cards for making their own versions of word reminders. She encourages students to keep the card visible on their desks or to use it as a bookmark. In whole-class and group lessons, Francine consistently asks students to review the word reminders when an unknown word is encountered in text.

Figure 5.1. Examples of Multiple Meanings Associated with the Word Craft

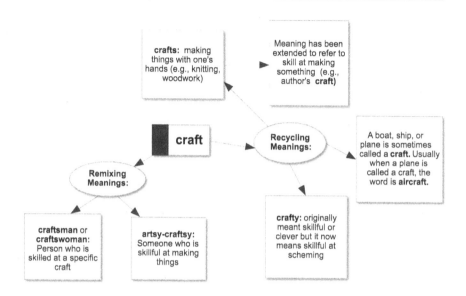

Figure 5.2. Word Reminders to Review and Remember

Word Networks: Words are part of families or networks. When you learn the members of word families or networks, your vocabulary grows.

Synonyms: Often, the meanings of words are connected to the meanings of other words. Many new words in books have meanings that are close to those of words you already know.

Morphology: Many words belong to families of words that have the same root words and meanings.

Multiple Meanings: Often, the same word has different meanings and uses. In different contexts, the meaning of a word can change.

Phrases: When a word is part of a compound word or a phrase, its meaning can change.

Word Origins: Many words in English come from French, which has a close connection to Spanish. The French/Spanish connection often gives clues about an English word's meaning.

Collections of Words

Following the first mini-lesson on multiple meanings of words, Francine puts up a chart where students can record words with multiple meanings. On the chart, students distinguish between multiple-meaning words that are used primarily in conversations and narratives and

Table 5.2. Examples of Multiple-Meaning Words

Multiple-Meaning Words with Common Meanings	Multiple-Meaning Words with Both Common and Specialized Meanings
bark, nails, jam, pool, mine, draft, squash, bolt, buckle, harbor, racket, hatch	force, compound, light, model, property, root, pole, light, current, plane, season, charge

those that also have specialized meanings in content areas. Some of the words on the chart in Francine's classroom appear in Table 5.2.

Choice Reading

Francine has collected a number of engaging books on the theme of multiple meanings. Some of the books in Table 5.3, such as the Fred Gwynne books, graphically depict potential confusions of different forms of words with multiple meanings or spellings. These books are sufficiently witty to keep her 4th-graders engaged. Students enjoyed Gwynne's books so much that they identified multiple-meaning words and created illustrations of these words.

Another group of students were inspired by Tabor's (2000) book of English idioms and their Spanish equivalents. Since several language groups are represented in Francine's classroom, these students collected familiar idioms, such as *easy as ABC* and *have second thoughts*, in various languages.

THE LAST WORD

Mastering multiple meanings of words does not occur from filling out numerous worksheets. Developing flexibility with words comes from reading, writing, and discussions. An astoundingly large number of vocabulary games and worksheets are available on Pinterest, on educational websites, and in educational products. Unfortunately, worksheets do not adequately explore how words take on unique meanings in the context of sentences. When learners are asked to distinguish between minimally different words (e.g., *to, too, two; buy, by, bye*), they can become confused and even make erroneous substitutions. A flexible use of vocabulary comes both from extensive reading and from conversations focused on the influences of different uses of words on the meaning of a text.

Table 5.3. Books That Illustrate the Recycling and Remixing Process

Category	Example of Title or Series
Stories where a character is confused by multiple meanings of words (including homonyms)	• *Amelia Bedelia* series (Parish & Parish, 1963)
Jokes for children, many derived from multiple meanings or noun–verb changes	• *Laugh-out-Loud Jokes for Kids* series (Elliott, 2010)
Word play with homonyms and homophones, although, at times, word play uses other features such as multiple meanings	• *Eight Ate* (Terban, 2007a) • *Dear Deer* (Baretta, 2010) • *If You Were a Homonym or a Homophone* (Loewen, 2007)
Word play that often uses a number of word changes, including multiple-meaning words and noun–verb shifts	• *The King Who Rained* (Gwynne, 1988) • A *Chocolate Moose for Dinner* (Gwynne, 1988) • *How Much Can a Bare Bear Bear?* (Cleary, 2014) • *See the Yak Yak* (Ghigna, 1999)
Word play that focuses on a single feature such as multiple meanings, compound words, or noun–verb changes	• *What's the Point? A Book About Multiple Meaning Words* (Fowler, 2010) • *Word Play* (Brunetti, 2017) • *Yaks Yak* (Park, 2016)
Idioms	• *Ve Lo Que Dices/See What You Say* (Tabor, 2000)

The Vocabulary Networks of Narrative Texts

Example 1: "First the look of despair faded out; then came a faint flush of hope; her eyes grew deep and bright as morning stars. The child was quite transfigured." (*Anne of Green Gables*, Montgomery, 1908)

Example 2: "...she wanted more calling than the goats, for the child was so excited and amused at the capers and lively games of her new playfellows that she saw and heard nothing else." (*Heidi*, Spyri, 1881)

These examples come from two of my favorite stories from childhood—the first reflecting my heritage as a child in Canada and the second reflecting my Swiss-German heritage. In both stories, an orphaned child transforms the grim world of adults. I wasn't an orphan, but my father had been orphaned as a young child, so I had a great interest in the plight of orphaned children. And I always loved—and still love—stories of transformation and the power of human goodness.

Stories are the repository of humankind's perspectives on possibilities and challenges. In *Anne of Green Gables* and *Heidi*, Anne and Heidi courageously solve their problems. Although the resolutions of all stories are not similarly positive, all stories do provide insight into the human condition.

This chapter is about the vocabulary that makes stories compelling and engaging for readers. The use of vocabulary in narrative texts differs from that in informational texts. Some features may not fit stereotypes about the complexity of narrative and informational texts. For example, narratives often have more rare words than informational texts. This feature of stories may seem counter to conventional wisdom, but all will become apparent in this chapter.

THE EVIDENCE

In a study of the rare words in narrative texts, Alia Pugh and I (2018) found four types of rare words. The types of rare words at three points of schooling are depicted in Figure 6.1.

> *Stories are the repository of humankind's perspectives on possibilities and challenges.*

A substantial number at each grade level were rare members of the 2,500 word families (e.g., *treeline, sunroom*). The other groups were new root words (e.g., *meek, incipient*), proper names (e.g., *Nome, Arapahoe*), and unusual words (e.g., *baa-baa*, an example of onomatopoeia).

Most of this chapter is devoted to the forms of rare words in narrative texts, as these are often the words that give narrative texts their distinctive style. However, the core vocabulary also is used in unique ways in narrative texts relative to its use in informational texts. I begin with a description of these distinctive uses of the core vocabulary and then devote the remainder of the chapter to the rare words in narrative texts.

Unique Uses of the Core Vocabulary in Narrative Textst

Core vocabulary continues to be prominent in narrative texts, as it is in all texts. The two introductory excerpts from *Anne* and *Heidi* reflect the usual pattern, wherein 90% or more of the words come from the core vocabulary. In the first excerpt, all but three of the words (i.e., *despair, flush, transfigured*) belong to the core vocabulary. But, as evident in the description of Anne's eyes as "deep and bright as morning stars," core vocabulary is not always used in a straightforward manner in narrative text. All of the words in this phrase are in the core vocabulary; however, in this setting, readers need to understand that these words are being used figuratively.

Figurative language. In figurative language, words—often appearing in phrases—have meanings that vary from their typical use. The techniques of figurative language are many, but the most common, especially in children's books, are metaphor, simile, and hyperbole. Table 6.1 presents descriptions and examples of each of these three common types of figurative language.

Even most primary-level students will be able to recognize the words in figurative phrases, since most use words in the core

Figure 6.1. Types of Rare Words in Narrative Texts

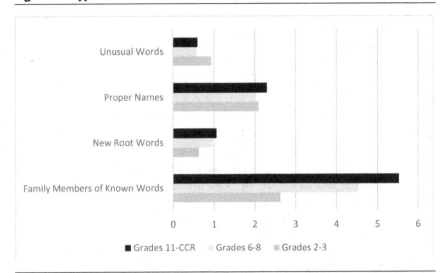

vocabulary. But when encountering phrases such as those in Table 6.1, students may interpret the meaning literally (although that would be hard to do in a story where crayons are leaving messages for a child!).

Idioms. Idioms are a form of figurative language that crosses over more frequently into everyday life. The language of conversations is filled with idiomatic language that is less formal than a simile like Yolen's (1987) "quiet as a dream" or Fletcher's (2003) "silent slippers." Hyperbole, such as the phrase "completely lose it" in *The Day the Crayons Quit* (Daywalt, 2013), is idiomatic in nature and also is likely to be present in children's oral language. Drawing children's attention to the presence of such idiomatic language in their lives teaches children about figurative language. Books that humorously illustrate idioms, such as *My Teacher Likes to Say* (Brennan-Nelson, 2004) and *In a Pickle* (Terban, 2007b), also support students in becoming aware of figurative language in general and idiomatic language in particular.

Whereas figurative language is unique to a given story and often lyrical in nature, idioms represent ideas that are familiar to members of a culture. This cultural specificity renders idioms incomprehensible on first reading or hearing by non-native English speakers. When teachers are alert to the challenges of idioms in conversations and in texts, they can discuss them with culturally and linguistically diverse students.

Table 6.1. Examples of Figurative Language in Children's Literature*

Type of Figurative Language	Definition	Example in Children's Literature
Metaphor	A word or phrase applied to an object or action to which it is not literally applicable	It comes up round, ripe, and huge over autumn fields of corn and wheat. Hello, harvest moon. *With silent slippers it climbs the night stairs.* (Fletcher, 2003, p. 4)
Simile	One thing compared with another thing of a different kind	And when their voices faded away it was *as quiet as a dream.* (Yolen, 1987, p. 2)
Hyperbole	Exaggerated statements that are not meant to be taken literally	If you DON'T START COLORING INSIDE the lines soon . . . I'm going to *COMPLETELY LOSE IT.* Your very neat friend, Purple Crayon (Daywalt, 2013, p. 5)

*The figurative language has been italicized.

The Rare Vocabulary of Narratives

A rich palette of vocabulary is a distinguishing feature of high-quality narratives, as illustrated by the following excerpt from a Caldecott winner—*Kitten's First Full Moon*:

> But Kitten only tumbled, bumping her nose and
> banging her ear and pinching her tail. Poor Kitten! (Henke, 2004)

In a single sentence, the kitten in Henke's tale tumbles, bumps, bangs, and pinches. The kitten's mishaps illustrate how the compelling storyline of a narrative comes alive through an array of words that are carefully chosen and rarely repeated.

Many words used to describe a character's actions (e.g., *tumbled* in *Kitten's First Full Moon*) or a character's trait or state of mind (e.g., *transfigured* in *Anne*) are rare in written language. Although these words may not have been encountered by students in texts previously, the concepts that these words represent are familiar to students. A quick reference to falling will be sufficient for 1st-graders to understand what *tumbling* means. Similarly, a comment about a rapid change should clarify the meaning of *transfigured* for 4th- and 5th-graders.

From the vantage of a single text, rare words may appear overwhelming. Across narrative texts, however, patterns in how authors use rare words can be identified. Awareness of two commonalities in the use of rare words in narratives can be especially helpful for students: (1) authors' use of rare words in developing elements of narratives, and (2) authors' choices of synonyms from concept clusters.

Rare words support development of narrative elements. Stories have an underlying structure or "grammar" that is built around specific elements (Stein, 1982). Not all stories have identical structures by any stretch of the imagination, but the underlying grammar of stories means that they share the elements of setting/time, main characters, problem, solution, and outcome. An author's use of rare words generally connects to these story elements. For example, the traits of individual characters figure heavily in the twists and turns of the plot of a story. When characters are resilient and energetic, as is the case with Anne and Heidi, readers anticipate the plot will take a particular direction. That is, the joy and hope of the young protagonists lead to the redemption of antagonistic or anxious characters (Grandfather in *Heidi* or the Cuthberts in *Anne*).

Alongside the characters, the most essential element of a story relates to the challenges the characters encounter; without challenges for characters to resolve, there is no story arc. In *Anne*, for example, the Cuthberts' impending problem of the substitution of a girl (and not just any girl, but Anne Shirley!) for a boy to help on their farm is conveyed in the last sentence of the first chapter: "[If Rachel Lynde] could have seen the child who was waiting patiently at the Bright River station at that very moment her pity would have been still deeper and more profound."

Rare words come from synonym networks with concepts known to students. Authors draw on semantic categories—networks or groups of words—to make particular traits and actions of characters vivid or to increase the drama of a problem. In Chapter 3, I described the 11 large groups of semantic categories to which all core vocabulary words belong. Four of the categories are filled with words that appear frequently in narrative texts—words having to do with the actions/movements, traits, communication, and emotions of characters. Each of these categories is populated with numerous words within the core vocabulary and beyond.

An example from the semantic category of emotions conveys the richness of the vocabulary of stories. Within this category are 110 words, including *sad, mad, hate,* and *worry.* Each of these words, in turn, is part of an extensive network of synonyms. When the word *sad* is entered into an online thesaurus, 46 words are identified, ranging from *morbid* to *gloomy.*

The size of these semantic networks in narrative texts becomes less intimidating for teachers, especially of primary-level students, when viewed from the perspective of the grade level at which words enter into the vocabulary of text. The idea of being *sad* is a concept with which kindergartners are familiar. Kindergartners are unlikely, however, to recognize *forlorn* or *disconsolate.* However, by the time these words appear in middle-grade or middle-school texts, students will have encountered numerous words within the network. Words such as *heartbroken, sorrowful,* and *gloomy* can be expected to appear in primary-level texts, giving students an anchor to understand more sophisticated forms of the concepts in the middle grades and onward.

To support teachers in lessons where students enlarge their networks of semantic categories, I identified a set of especially rich semantic networks in narrative texts: communication, emotions, movement, and traits. Table 6.2 provides key words from these groups. A lesson is provided around each of these words in an online resource called Super Synonym Sets for Stories (Synonym Sets) at TextProject.org.

An illustrative semantic map for one of the key words in the Synonym Sets—*sad*—is provided in Figure 6.2. A handful of the words in this semantic cluster, such as *unhappy* and *depressed,* are in the core vocabulary, but others, like *despondent* and *inconsolable,* are not.

Not all the words on a semantic map like that in Figure 6.2 are intended to be provided to students of all ages or on a single occasion. But over time, this resource can support growth in students' semantic networks for recurring concepts in stories. When students understand that the rare words in stories often represent concepts with which they are familiar, they can tackle unknown words with confidence.

Proper names are a prominent form of rare words. In revisiting the depiction of rare word types in Figure 6.1, you will see that proper names make up the second biggest source of rare words in narrative texts. Despite the importance of proper names in stories, there are few insights from research as to how difficult these words are for students to recognize. What is clear, though, is that proper names form a unique

Table 6.2. Key Words at the Center of Prolific Semantic Clusters in Narrative Texts*

Communication/ Internal Processes (verbs)	Emotions (adjectives, nouns, and verbs)	Movement (verbs)	Traits (adjectives)
think	glad	go	funny
argue	sad	send	smart
observe	mad	start	brave
guess	hope	stop	selfish
say	fear	stay	shy

*From Super Synonym Sets for Stories, TextProject.org

class of vocabulary. Some proper names have common meanings (e.g., Heather, Robin), but most are not part of morphological families, such as the names of Grandfather's two goats in *Heidi*: Schwanli and Baerli. For most American students, the pro-

> *Students can struggle with pronunciations of names and then, when a text is dense with unpronounceable names, become disengaged.*

nunciation of these names in their original Swiss German will be challenging. And—as is the case with many names—the meaning of these words in the language of origin is not evident (Schwanli means Little Swan; Baerli means Little Bear).

Proper names can be the rare words that are repeated most often in stories. This repetition is both bad news and good news for readers. The bad news is that students can struggle with pronunciations of names and then, when a text is dense with unpronounceable names, become disengaged. The good news is that when proper names are associated with specific characters, the repetition of these words means that the burden of new words is lessened.

There is much teachers can do to help students who struggle with unfamiliar proper names. First, by minimizing correction of students' pronunciations in oral reading contexts, teachers can reduce challenges with proper names in narrative texts. Teachers also can support students in differentiating the traits associated with characters in stories, especially in long texts. For example, Rachel Lynde and Marilla Cuthbert are two strong female characters in *Anne* who both make tart and acerbic comments at the beginning of the book. As the story progresses, Marilla's expressions soften, while Rachel's comments

Figure 6.2. Semantic Map for the Synonym Network of Sad

S4-13

Sad

Sad as in full of grief
- sorrow
- remorse
- despondent
- inconsolable
- depressed
- gloomy
- downcast
- downhearted
- melancholy
- morose
- unhappy
- miserable
- cheerless
- heartbroken
- blue
- glum

Sad as in bad quality
- pathetic
- terrible
- sorry
- deplorable
- run-down
- shabby
- bleak
- horrible
- inferior
- poor

THE SPANISH CONNECTION
- horrible / horrible
- melancholy / melancolía
- inconsolable / inconsolable

Sad

COMMON PHRASES
- Sad face
- Sad situation

IDIOMS
- Sad song
- Beyond all hope
- Sad/sorry sight
- A sad state
- Sadder but wiser
- (Feeling) blue

remain contentious. Using proper names to differentiate characters is an important part of story comprehension.

Narrative texts have numerous unusual words. The unusual words referred to in Figure 6.1 encompass colloquial language, era-specific vocabulary, onomatopoeia, interjections, and abbreviations. The presence of these groups varies at different grade levels. Colloquial language rarely is used in the primary grades, while onomatopoeia is a relatively frequent technique in the primary grades and is virtually absent in the upper grades.

Colloquial and era-specific language. Narrative texts are distinguished from most informational texts by the presence of dialogue. When authors attempt to replicate the casualness of spoken language in narratives, they often use colloquial language (Sornig, 1981). Colloquial language is defined as informal, everyday, and conversational. The nature of colloquial language is evident in the excerpts from *M. C. Higgins, the Great* (Hamilton, 1974) in Table 6.3, in which characters often use variant grammatical patterns ("Wish I had me a gun") in dialogue.

A more dramatic form of colloquial language occurs when authors replicate the sounds as well as the grammatical patterns of different dialects. Burnett (1911), in *The Secret Garden*, made substantial use of the Yorkshire dialect. Deciphering the meaning of the sentence "An' tha's browt th' young 'un with thee," will likely be challenging for many 21st-century American students. Texts where authors use dialect frequently require sensitivity and scaffolding by teachers.

The Birchbark House (Erdrich, 2002) illustrates another unique form of vocabulary in some books—words from a language other than English. A glossary of Ojibwa words provides support in *The Birchbark House*, but such an aid is not included in all texts with non-English words. When the non-English words in texts come from languages that are spoken by students in the classroom, an outstanding opportunity exists for capitalizing on students' knowledge. Teachers should bear in mind, however, that some native speakers of languages other than English have not had the chance to become literate in their native language. In such cases, technology that gives pronunciations of words in other languages can be used to create connections.

The examples in Table 6.3 also illustrate words associated with different time periods. In *The Secret Garden* (Burnett, 1911), British colonization in India, long sea voyages, and diseases such as typhoid are part of the backstory of Mary, the protagonist. Words such as *pinafores* and *shilling* refer to items common at the beginning of the 20th century but not in 21st-century America.

M. C. Higgins, the Great (see Table 6.3), in common with other books that have become classics, represents a culture and time period that were unfamiliar to many children in urban and suburban locations even when it was published in 1974. Frequently, the first chapter of a book or the first paragraph of a short story is laden with words related to place and time. When teachers are sensitive to this initial load on vocabulary, they can support students who may feel overwhelmed by the rare and often unusual vocabulary.

Interjections, onomatopoeia, and abbreviations. Most of the words in the unusual word category in Figure 6.1 for grades 2 and 3 were interjections or onomatopoeia. Interjections are words expressing sudden or intense emotions, such as surprise (Oh!) or distaste (Ugh!). These expressions are almost always grammatically distinct, typically followed by an exclamation mark (hence, these terms also are called exclamations).

Onomatopoeia refers to vocally graphic representations of sounds, such as those associated with animals (e.g., *meow*), machines (e.g., *vroom-vroom*), explosions (e.g., *pop*), weather (e.g., *plip plop*), and people (e.g., *burp*). In read-alouds of texts, onomatopoeia and interjections create interest and variety. Researchers have yet to study how young readers respond to these words when reading independently.

The appearances of onomatopoeia and interjections were few among the unusual words in texts at the middle- and high-school levels. The unusual words represented in Figure 6.1 at the upper levels were primarily abbreviations. Common abbreviations such as *Mr.,* *Ms., Mrs.,* and *Dr.* need to be read as the entire word, even though all letters are not present. Acronyms need to be understood as representing individual words (e.g., UNICEF), although some acronyms have become unique words (e.g., *scuba, radar*). The study of abbreviations in reading is beginning to be of some interest to scholars as a result of instant messaging (Plester, Wood, & Joshi, 2009). As is the case with most of the forms of unusual language in this section, however, students' ability to negotiate these forms when reading remains largely uninvestigated. As with colloquial and era-specific language, the best advice to teachers is to be sensitive to unusual forms of language, especially when students are English learners or struggling readers.

Table 6.3. Colloquialisms and Unusual Vocabulary in Grades 4–5 Narrative Texts*

Title	Colloquialism	Rare Words Related to Time and/or Place	Context
Bud, Not Buddy (Curtis, 2001)	• he was swole up • those Amoses wouldn't've even tried to pull the roach out • The boss cop said, "You lily-livered rats"	cur double-barreled locomotive Ticonderoga urchins vermin yellow-jacket Shantytown Hooverville	1936 in midwestern United States
M. C. Higgins, the Great (Hamilton, 1974)	• "You should of gone before she waked," M. C. said. • "Wish I had me a gun," he said.	cirque dappled holler outcroppings thicket	Subcultures in Appalachian Mountains in 1960s when effects of strip mining were becoming apparent
The Secret Garden (Burnett, 1911)	• "Well enow. Th' carriage is waitin' outside for thee." • An' tha's browt th' young 'un with thee."	Ayah brougham cinders embroidered hearth marmalade missel moor pinafores scullerymaid shilling treacle turrets vicarage victuals whitewashed	Late-19th-century Great Britain on an estate in an isolated part of Yorkshire

* Texts come from the list of exemplars for grades 4 and 5 in the CCSS.

SMALL CHANGES = BIG RESULTS

For many of Reggie's 3rd-grade students in an urban school, the language of narratives can vary considerably from the conversations that they hear on the playground or even on television shows. Reggie knows that his students will need strong vocabularies to be successful with middle-grade texts such as those listed in Table 6.3. He recognizes that his students need to have strategies for dealing with unknown proper names and synonyms from prolific networks. Another of Reggie's goals is to support informed expectations on the part of his students about the types of rare words they will encounter in narrative texts. Reggie has made small changes in conversations, collections of words, and core and choice reading in order to increase his students' proficiency with the vocabulary of narrative texts.

Conversations

Reggie's students have been learning about bar graphs in mathematics, which makes the presentation of a bar graph depicting rare words in 2nd- and 3rd-grade texts (see Figure 6.1) a perfect context for conversations about how words work. He has selected texts from his English/Language Arts program (Afflerbach et al., 2013) to illustrate the presence of particular kinds of rare vocabulary, such as the examples in Table 6.4.

In these conversations, Reggie asks groups of students to read different sections of the same text to identify rare words. As results are shared, Reggie and his students address similarities and differences in the types of rare words across a text. For example, do specific challenging words reappear across the text? Or, if there is considerable variety in rare words, can students detect similarities in the meanings or purposes of words?

Collections of Words

Reggie uses the words that cluster around the prolific synonyms listed in Table 6.2—words such as *argue, sad, send,* and *smart*—as the basis for word collections. He consults the Super Synonym Sets for Stories at TextProject.org to identify anchor words for a collection. For example, he places two examples of differing meanings of *sad* (see Figure 6.2)—*unhappy* (full of grief) and *poor* (bad quality) to start students

Table 6.4. Examples of Texts with Types of Rare Words*

Type of Rare Word	Text Title	Text Excerpt
Proper names	*Atlantis: The Legend of a Lost City* (Balit, 1999)	In the center of the island there stood a mountain, and at the foot of the mountain lived a man called **Evenor** and his wife, **Leucippe.** They lived happily together, working hard to tend the **barren** land, and brought up their daughter **Cleito** to honor all creatures.
Compound words	*Prudy's Problem: And How She Solved It* (Armstrong-Ellis, 2002)	She had collections of **ribbons, shoelaces, souvenir** postcards, flowered **fabric scraps,** pencils with fancy ends, pink **scarves** with orange **polka** dots, old calendars, salt and pepper shakers with faces, dried-out **erasers,** plastic **lizards**, pointy sunglasses, china animals, heart-shaped candy boxes with the paper candy cups still inside . . .
Unusual words	*Happy Birthday Mr. Kang* (Roth, 2001)	**"Shhhh!"** says Mr. **Kang** and Sam, but they wait as she closes the door. Mrs. Kang takes one extra minute to slip two warm **almond** cakes into Sam's pocket.
New root words	*When Charlie McButton Lost Power* (Collins, 2005)	Somehow his head didn't warn of his **folly,** and Charlie **McButton**. . . . He **pounced** on that dolly. He **plucked** out his prize through the baby doll's dress. And **Isabel** Jane made a sound of **distress.** It was just a short walk to the foot of the stair where **resided** the McButton time-out chair.

*Rare words are in boldfaced type.

in collecting synonyms. Once words related to a definition have been collected, Reggie encourages students to sort the words according to a semantic gradient (Blachowicz & Fisher, 2006), which is a group of semantically related words that are placed along a continuum according to shades of meaning. For example, words related to *sorrow* might range from *grief-stricken* to *despondent* to *downcast*.

Core Reading

When examples of figurative language appear in the texts of the school's core reading program, Reggie draws students' attention to the figures of speech. But for specific instruction on figurative language, he uses texts that bring to the foreground a specific figurative-language technique. For similes, he uses *Quick as a Cricket* (Wood, 1982); for hyperbole, *The Day the Crayons Quit* (Daywalt, 2013); and for metaphor, *If I Were a Lion* (Weeks, 2007). Many of Reggie's students are familiar with these books from kindergarten or 1st grade. And he knows that these texts are especially effective; the specific techniques are sufficiently clear to students so that they are able to create their own illustrations and descriptions of figurative language.

Reggie uses books such as Wallace Edwards's *The Cat's Pajamas* (2010) and *Monkey Business* (2013) to teach about idioms. The illustrations of a bear playing violin with a noodle ("He was forced to use his noodle)" or of a crab tying the bowtie for a giraffe ("She could always be counted on in a pinch") are silly and memorable. These books have inspired Reggie's students to create their own books of idioms—books that have been a source of hilarity and engagement. To find additional idioms, Reggie and his students have drawn on the *Scholastic Dictionary of Idioms* (Terban, 2006) and The Phrase Finder, a website (www.phrases.org.uk) that distinguishes between American and British idioms.

Choice Reading

Support from teachers on the types of books that are available can lay the foundation for the lifelong reading that is the goal of English/Language Arts instruction. Table 6.5 provides recommendations that Reggie offers to his students. His intention is not that his list be the sole source of book recommendations for choice reading, but he knows that a menu of choices can uncover new options for some students. By increasing his students' exposure to genres, authors, and topics, Reggie ensures that his students develop bodies of knowledge and habits of lifelong reading.

> *By increasing his students' exposure to genres, authors, and topics, Reggie ensures that his students develop bodies of knowledge and habits of lifelong reading.*

Table 6.5. Examples of Recommendations of Narrative Texts for 3rd-Graders' Choice Reading

Genre	Titles (Author)
Mysteries	*Howliday Inn* (Howe, 2012)
	Inspector Flytrap (Angeleberger, 2016)
	Nooks and Crannies (Lawson, 2016)
	Murilla Gorilla, Jungle Detective (Lloyd, 2013)
Stories About Our Country	*John F. Kennedy: America's Youngest President* (Frisbee, 1986)
	Moonwalk: The First Trip to the Moon (Donnelly, 1989)
	The Secret Soldier: The Story of Deborah Sampson (McGovern, 1990)
	Rosa Parks (Greenfield, 1995
Stories About Families	*How My Family Lives in America* (Kuklin, 1998)
	Mama, I'll Give You the World (Schotter, 2006)
	My Name Is Maria Isabel (Ada, 1993)
	Pop's Bridge (Bunting, 2006)
Fantasy: Past and Future	*The Knights of the Kitchen Table* (Scieszka, 1998)
	Lug, Blast from the North (Zeltser, 2016)
	Zita the Spacegirl (Hatke, 2014)
	Aliens for Breakfast (Spinner, 2011)

THE LAST WORD

An increased emphasis on knowledge building in English/Language Arts periods should not be misconstrued to mean a lack of attention to narrative texts. The assignment of percentages to text genres (with a high percentage devoted to informational texts) within the Common Core State Standards (NGACBP & CCSSO, 2010b) could contribute to such an interpretation. But such an interpretation would be inaccurate. Much knowledge about human experiences, geographic contexts, and historical periods comes from narrative texts. Students develop essential bodies of knowledge through their reading of narrative texts. Indeed, psychological experiments have shown that people retain information in deeper ways when they need to make inferences in narrative texts than when the information is explicitly stated, as often occurs in informational texts (Chabris & Simons, 2011). Memory is enhanced by richness of experience; when engaging narratives include descriptions of places that students have never seen or experiences that they are unlikely to have, readers are more likely to retain knowledge from these stories. Stories, old and new, are a source of enjoyment. They also can be the source of deep and broad knowledge about the world—past, present, and visions of the future.

CHAPTER 7

The Vocabulary Networks of Informational Texts

Example 1: Nesting in this barren, ice-covered world isn't a problem because emperors don't build nests. The male incubates the one-pound egg on his feet, covering it with a featherless fold of skin called a "brood patch." ("Daddy Day Care," Musgrave, 2004)

Example 2: In the past when scientists studied mummies, they had to cut through the body, or unwrap it. Today, they can explore inside a mummy while it is whole. Using x-ray scanners, researchers can produce 3-D images of a mummy's insides. ("Unwrapping the Past," Smith, 2007)

The two texts from which these introductory excerpts come were used on a recent National Assessment of Educational Progress (NAEP), which often is referred to as the national report of American students' performances at specific points in time. In the late 1960s, the NAEP reading assessment made no distinction in text type. Since then, the content of the NAEP reading assessment has shifted in favor of informational texts. At present, half of the texts in grade 4, 55% in grade 8, and 70% in high school are informational (National Assessment Governing Board, 2015). Common Core State Standards developers targeted the same percentages for students' learning experiences in English/Language Arts (ELA) classes (NGACBP & CCSSO, 2010b).

Often, publishers advertise high percentages of informational texts in their ELA core reading programs. The presence of informational texts in an ELA program, however, serves a much greater purpose than merely hitting target percentages. Informational texts are central to achieving a primary purpose of the ELA program: to develop the background knowledge that underlies comprehension of all texts.

THE EVIDENCE

The movement of informational text from a somewhat peripheral to a central role in ELA periods raises numerous questions for teachers. Why do policymakers and researchers recommend this shift? Are the topics addressed by informational text exactly the same as those in the state content-area standards at specific grade levels? In particular, what does this shift mean for vocabulary instruction in ELA periods? In this chapter, I address the whys and whats of the emphasis on informational texts in ELA and then go on to describe what a focus on informational text means for vocabulary instruction.

Why Informational Text in ELA?

If a single finding were to be identified as the most definitive conclusion from the past 50 years of reading research, it would be that knowledge about a topic strongly predicts comprehension (Ahmed et al., 2016; Alexander, Kulikowich, & Schulze, 1994). If students are not familiar with penguins or the frigid cold of Antarctica, they will have a difficult time comprehending "Daddy Day Care" (excerpted at the beginning of the chapter). If students know nothing about mummies, "Unwrapping the Past" (also at the beginning of the chapter) will be a challenge to understand.

This finding on the role of background knowledge in comprehension has inspired teachers to do guided walk-throughs of text prior to students' reading. In these walk-throughs, teachers point out salient information, including vocabulary, that they believe will support students' comprehension. But what happens when students read on their own? For example, if passages on the unique behaviors of Emperor penguins or on mummies have not been included in the curriculum, how will students respond when presented with texts they need to read independently, such as "Daddy Day Care" and "Unwrapping the Past"?

The answer to this question is that students struggle in comprehending on their own. The National Report Card, which summarizes the performance of American students on the NAEP, shows that the comprehension of American students has not kept pace with the increased demands on literacy over the past decades (National Center for Education Statistics, 2017). Oral reading fluency levels have increased (Hasbrouck & Tindal, 2017), but comprehension levels have not.

The bottom line is that teachers simply cannot give students all the background knowledge they need for a lifetime of reading. Students need to be taught how to draw on prior knowledge and related vocabulary of topics. If students' knowledge of a topic is sparse, they need to know how to make hypotheses about the text content and to figure out pertinent topic-related vocabulary in the text. The integral relationship between background knowledge and comprehension of any text—including narrative ones—means that a text diet of solely narrative texts over the elementary years is unlikely to develop the necessary strategies or reservoirs of background knowledge. Reviews of the content in ELA periods confirm that the texts of instruction can flit from topic to topic (Brenner & Hiebert, 2010). All the while, the time devoted to science and social studies in elementary school has decreased. The push for an increased presence of informational text in ELA periods emanates from the view that building background knowledge is an essential part of the ELA curriculum.

Learning to learn from texts is a process that begins early in children's reading experiences. This process is not delayed until students are proficient readers. Texts that support beginning readers in learning short vowel patterns, for example, can describe things that pigs like to do, such as sit in the mud and swim in water, or describe the purposes of different kinds of transportation, such as trucks, vans, and buses (Hiebert, 2012). When a foundation in knowledge is recognized as fundamental to comprehension of all texts, including narrative ones, informational texts become a valued and essential part of the ELA curriculum.

> *Learning to learn from texts is a process that begins early in children's reading experiences.*

What Informational Texts in ELA?

The reasons for the central role of informational text and its vocabulary in the ELA classroom are evident. But a persistent issue pertains to the knowledge domains that should be the focus of ELA. Policies related to the increased presence of informational texts, in both ELA curriculum and assessments, have led to a random assortment of topics in many literacy programs now on the market. The focus has been on achieving targeted percentages of informational texts rather than on the knowledge that students are gaining. In one widely used leveled text program (Reading A–Z, n.d.), the informational texts for the 3rd-grade level address such disparate topics as birds of prey, Maremma sheepdogs that protect penguins, the authenticity of the Mona Lisa, and an abandoned copper mine.

No state or national standards for ELA recommend the appropriate knowledge domains for particular grade levels; rather the standards focus on strategies and skills. Consider a typical standard for Reading of Informational Text in the Common Core State Standards (NGACBP & CCSSO, 2010a): "Compare and contrast the most important points and key details presented in two texts on the same topic" (p. 8). This standard begs the question of which topics should be the focus of such discussions. Will any topic do? A comparison of two articles on the role of Maremma sheepdogs? A comparison of two articles on the sources of drought in the West?

Another question that arises is whether ELA is now an umbrella for instruction of social studies and science. That is, does the critical role of informational text in ELA mean that there is no science and social studies instruction? The specific content of ELA informational texts may not be clearly defined, but the answer to the question of a sustaining role for social studies and science instruction is unequivocal: An emphasis on informational text in ELA classes is not a substitute for content-area instruction. Reading a text on mummification where scientists use 3-D imaging, as in Example 2 at the beginning of this chapter, does not take the place of a demonstration of digital light processing in a science class. Building a 3-D image and accompanying 3-D glasses involves discussions and explanations that extend beyond the mentioning of the 3-D imaging process in an article on mummies. Texts are used for reference in content-area projects; students record and write about their experiments and observations in notebooks. Content-area and ELA experiences benefit from integration, but content-area instruction is not limited to reading texts.

However, this response still does not answer the question, "What content should be the focus of ELA instruction?" At TextProject.org, my colleagues and I have used state standards in subject areas and a review of subject areas that are steadily disappearing from the school day, such as music, dance, drama, architecture, visual arts, and health, to identify topics for creating and curating texts. As illustrated in Table 7.1, we also emphasize topics of interest to children and young adolescents—sports, fashion, and biographies of heroes. The list in Table 7.1 should not be taken as a mandate but rather as an illustration of a matrix for building an ELA topic-based curriculum. Teachers should also remember that the purpose of a focused set of topics is for students to develop

Table 7.1. Topic Matrix for Text Selection at TextProject.org

Child-Friendly Title	Content Area
Making Beautiful Things: Art, Fashion, & Movies	Fine Arts
Blast from the Past	History
Designing & Inventing: Engineering & Architecture	Physical Science
Heroes and Famous People	History/Human Interest
How Things Work: On Earth & in Space	Physical Science & Astronomy
Learning About Myself, Friends, & Family	Social and Emotional Learning
Making and Celebrating Communities	Culture/Civics
Rhymes and Rhythm: Poetry & Music	Literature and Fine Arts
Health and Sports	Life Sciences
Stories We Tell: New & Old	Literature and Social/Emotional Learning
The Living World: Habitats, Animals, & Weather	Life Sciences
Travel and Places	Geography

expertise in learning how to use texts to learn, not for ensuring that every possible topic under the sun has been covered.

The Features of Vocabulary in Informational Texts

Particular groups of words in the core vocabulary—like high-function words—act in similar ways in informational texts as in narrative texts. But there are differences in the prominence of some of the word families in the core vocabulary. For example, one set of words described as general academic words takes on an increasingly more visible role in informational texts across the grades. As would be expected because of the emphasis on content, the rare words in informational text come from semantic networks of words that often do not appear frequently in narrative texts.

Key words fit into topic networks. The concepts represented by the critical words in informational text are interconnected in meaning, not interchangeable synonyms as is the case in narrative text. The network of words from the article "Unwrapping the Past" (Example 2) is

Figure 7.1. Map of the Critical Vocabulary in "Unwrapping the Past"

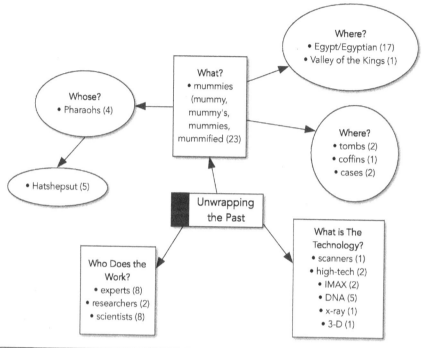

illustrated in the graphic in Figure 7.1. Each of the rectangular boxes represents a different set of ideas, but these ideas are interrelated and linked conceptually. Only as students create relationships between the words in topic-specific networks do they gain understandings of complex concepts.

The target words are repeated. Concepts in informational text are often less familiar to students than concepts in narrative text, but the good news is that the topic-specific words often are repeated. The numbers following the words in Figure 7.1 represent the number of repetitions of words across the entire passage from which Example 2 comes. When authors of informational texts are intent on communicating content on specific aspects of a topic, they use the content-specific vocabulary over and over again. The author of "Daddy Day Care" refers to Emperor penguins frequently (11 times in the entire passage from which Example 1 comes). The purpose of the article is to distinguish the unique paternal behaviors of the Emperor penguin.

Consequently, the author consistently uses the term Emperor penguin, not "cuddly creature" or "flightless seabird," as might be the case in a story about a stranded penguin. Repetition of unique vocabulary can make informational texts especially conducive to the development of automaticity in recognizing vocabulary. A word may not make sense to the reader the first time it appears, but with varying uses, the meaning becomes clearer.

Topic-specific vocabulary often occurs in phrases and has multiple meanings. Chapter 5 was devoted to the topic of recycling (words taking on different meanings) and remixing (words being used in complex phrases with specialized meanings). It is in informational texts that these features are especially prevalent. In particular, the reason for describing open compounds in content as complex phrases was described. In conversational and narrative language, the meanings of open compounds such as *free sample* or *free throw* are fairly straightforward. In content areas, however, sets of words that consistently appear together can have unique and complex meanings. A *free press*, for example, does not refer to a machine or materials that require no payment, but rather to a body of media that is not controlled or restricted by government censorship.

As scholarship on a topic deepens, the phrases in content areas can become increasingly more complex. Such is the case as scientists have learned more about deriving cells from living matter. First, the term *stem cell* was used to distinguish it from a cell or specialized human cell. More investigations have led to distinctions in the kinds of stem cells—embryonic stem cells, somatic stem cells, tissue-specific stem cells, mesenchymal stem cells, and induced pluripotent stem cells. With further scientific investigation, even more fine-tuned distinctions in the vocabulary related to stem cells can be expected in the future.

Supporting students in treating certain sets or groups of words as a single concept rather than as individual words is essential to success in comprehending text in all content areas. Table 5.1 offers examples of complex phrases from mathematics (e.g., *place value*), social studies (e.g., *capital resources*), and science (*change of state*). R. J. Marzano and Simms (2011) found that 25% or more of the vocabulary in content areas was made up of complex phrases. As students and teachers construct semantic networks of the vocabulary in content areas, attention to how complex phrases rely on and connect ideas on a topic should be a priority.

Numerous words in content areas also have multiple meanings, including words that are used in everyday conversation with meanings that may be less technical or precise than their meanings in content areas. For example, when the word *mass* appears in chemistry, its meaning is somewhat similar to the everyday meaning (having to do with amount), but is sufficiently distinctive (having to do with the matter of an object) that students can find it hard to assimilate the new meaning (Cervetti, Hiebert, Pearson, & McClung, 2015). The challenge of multiple-meaning words only intensifies when a word has unique meanings across several content areas. Consider just a few of the uses of the word *cell* in different content areas:

Physical science: dry cell, electrochemical cell, solar cell
Civics and social studies: terrorist cell, sleeper cell, prison cell
Biology: prokaryotic cell, stem cell
Telecommunications: cellular region, cellular/cell phone
Computing: cell statistics

When words with common meanings have specialized meanings in content areas, teachers need to be sensitive to the potential for confusion. Discussions in which the different meanings are made explicit can support students in making the necessary distinctions.

Proper names are prominent—and can be the content. Two kinds of proper names are prominent in informational texts: content-related proper names and proper names of experts. The first kind of proper name constitutes an essential part of the topic. For example, "Unwrapping the Past" is about the use of new technologies to identify the remains of the Pharaoh Hatshepsut. Proper names such as Hatshepsut and Ancient Egypt are central to this discussion. In "Daddy Day Care," the species of penguin—Emperor—and its habitat—Antarctica—are central to the content. The males of all penguin species do not display the same caregiving behaviors as those of the Emperor penguin, which makes the name of the species critical to the content of the passage.

A second kind of proper name appears frequently in magazine articles—the names and affiliations of experts on a topic. The credentials of an expert are used to substantiate or illustrate a claim in an article. In a section of "Unwrapping the Past," a principal investigator in producing and studying the 3-D images of Pharaoh Hatshepsut's mummy is identified as Bob Brier from Long Island University in New York. Brier is quoted as describing the benefits of high-tech techniques, which were not available in the past, in verifying the identity of a mummy. The comments of experts can add to an understanding of the topic. Further, the credentials of experts need to be evaluated for veracity of an argument or claim. Unlike the proper names of historical figures or species, however, the names of experts are unlikely to appear in subsequent texts. That is, some proper names in a text are not as critical to remember as others. Guidance from teachers on the distinction between these two groups of proper names in informational texts can be useful for students.

General academic vocabulary can be extensive in informational texts. Words such as compare, form, and consists have been given the label of general academic vocabulary (Hiebert & Lubliner, 2008). These words often are ignored in ELA vocabulary instruction, where words unique to narratives (e.g., blurted, mascot) take precedence. Even with the recent increase of informational texts in ELA curriculum, general academic vocabulary can be overshadowed by topic-specific words. For example, the words identified for instruction in an informational text, *Life on the Ice* (Goodman, 2006), in a core reading program (Baumann et al., 2014) include words related to the text's topic (e.g., region, climate, shelter), while general academic words (e.g., explain, problem, solve) that appear in the same text are not targeted for vocabulary instruction. However, general academic words are used frequently in texts and in descriptions of activities in schools, including assessments.

General academic vocabulary can be an obstacle in students' comprehension, especially that of English learners (Cummins, 1986), for several reasons. First and foremost, these words are abstract and can be used in ambiguous ways. Words like *form* or *model*, which are sometimes verbs and sometimes nouns, typify multiple-meaning words.

Second, many general academic words occur primarily in texts and do not figure heavily in conversations. When these words do occur in conversations, their meanings are not necessarily as precise as their meanings in texts. In a conversation, the statement, "You need to be an example for your brother," refers to being a role model, although the specific meaning of *example* is left unsaid. By contrast, when students are asked to "give an example of where it is better to use percents than fractions" in mathematics, they are expected to identify a specific illustration or case.

A third challenge lies in the multisyllabic nature of many general academic words. A two-syllable word such as *renew* may not be a problem, but when two syllables are added to make *renewable* and another syllable is added to make *nonrenewable*, the likelihood that struggling readers will attempt to comprehend the word decreases. Distributing lists of general academic words such as the Academic Word List (Coxhead, 2000) for students to learn will do little to support their facility with these words in content-area texts. Rather, general academic words should be taught in the context of sentences and as members of morphological families.

SMALL CHANGES = BIG RESULTS

Devin, a 5th-grade teacher, has been working hard to prepare his students for middle school. He knows that next year his students will be in content-specialty classes where expectations for literacy proficiency are high. Devin's focus has been on making small changes that give his students the chance to develop areas of expertise within content areas, including ones that often are pushed to the background in the school curriculum, such as the arts and music.

Conversations

Devin has made small changes in classroom conversations so that his 5th-graders can share the knowledge that they gain from texts. When preparing for a transition in the school day (e.g., going to lunch, changing content areas), Devin asks his students to describe new information that they have gained from their reading. Devin has explored a variety of formats in which students can share their expertise and related vocabulary with their classmates. For example, at the end of a quarter, he asks students to recommend a book or an article from their choice reading for their peers.

Another activity, Be an Expert, has proven to be especially compelling for Devin's students. A board in his classroom is used exclusively for students to post graphics or illustrations of what they have learned through reading extensively on a topic. Figure 7.2 gives an example of an Expert board in Devin's classroom—Lyn's display of pictures related to Mozart. Lyn was intrigued, when she read *Naturally Wild Musicians* (Christie, 2007), to learn of Mozart's attachment to

Figure 7.2. Lyn's Expert Summary on Mozart

a starling, which led her to read more about Mozart as well as stories about contemporary musicians, such as *John's Secret Dreams: The John Lennon Story* (Rappaport, 2004).

Jack has become the acknowledged mathematical expert in the classroom, as evident in his display of the Fibonacci sequence in nature, shown in Figure 7.3. His expertise began with his reading of *The Number Devil: A Mathematical Adventure* (Enzensberger, 2000) and has extended to a biography of Leonardo of Pisa (the mathematician who identified the Fibonacci sequence) and several books on Fibonacci numbers in nature.

Core Reading

Devin read about the Article-a-Day initiative (Hiebert, 2018), in which a set of articles on a topic is read over 1 or 2 weeks. This initiative, Devin was convinced, would support both breadth in topics (as many as a dozen or more topics can be covered during the school year) and depth on specific topics (typically six articles are provided per topic).

Figure 7.3. Jack's Expert Summary on Fibonacci Patterns

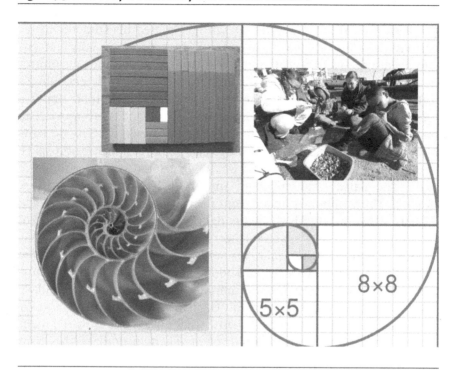

Devin found the small change of adding a 10-minute period of daily article reading easy to implement because of an open-access website that sponsors the Article-a-Day initiative: ReadWorks.org. This nonprofit organization has well over 4,500 articles (as of mid-2019) that cover a range of grades and text complexity levels—all available for free use. The articles are tagged for content and comprehension strategies (e.g., cause-and-effect, main ideas) and have accompanying comprehension and vocabulary activities. Further, teachers can access approximately 500 topics (again, as of mid-2019), each with six or more articles.

What has impressed Devin about the Article-a-Day resources at ReadWorks.org is their accessibility and comprehensiveness. But he is also aware that, on particular topics of interest, other organizations, including government agencies and nonprofits (e.g., Text-Project.org), can support his students in pursuing a topic in greater depth.

Collections of Words

For each topical set of articles, Devin has guided his students in recording their knowledge on a semantic map. He especially has encouraged students to revisit their semantic maps when they encounter new material on a topic. Devin models the process of refreshing a semantic map after acquiring new information, using a topic that has recurred in the Article-a-Day initiative—space and astronomy. The map in Figure 7.4 illustrates the changes that Devin and his students have made in the class map as they read additional articles on space and astronomy. The vocabulary from the first set of articles around the topic "The Galaxy and Universe" appears in Figure 7.4 without any shading. The vocabulary added from the second set of articles on "The Fathers of Astronomy" is shaded in light gray, while the third group of words from the topic "Space Science" appears in darker gray.

Devin revisits the topical maps periodically since students can lose sight of what they have learned. These maps are a good source for students to review content and the manner in which topical vocabulary is connected. During these sessions, Devin asks students to share their semantic maps with partners. In pairs, students explain how the main points relate to one another and how details help to make the main points clearer.

Choice Reading

Devin's efforts in building the breadth and depth of his students' background knowledge are not limited to magazine articles. Together with his students, he has worked hard to identify trade books that pertain to topics in his curriculum. Devin recognizes that students need to have opportunities to select their own topics and texts, but he also knows that many of his students become perplexed as to what to read next. Further, he wants to demonstrate to students the benefits of developing areas of expertise. Part of the evolving list of trade books identified by Devin and his students appears in Figure 7.5.

THE LAST WORD

The message about the critical role of background knowledge in comprehending is not new. It has been conveyed in numerous workshops,

Figure 7.4. The Growth of a Topical Map over Time

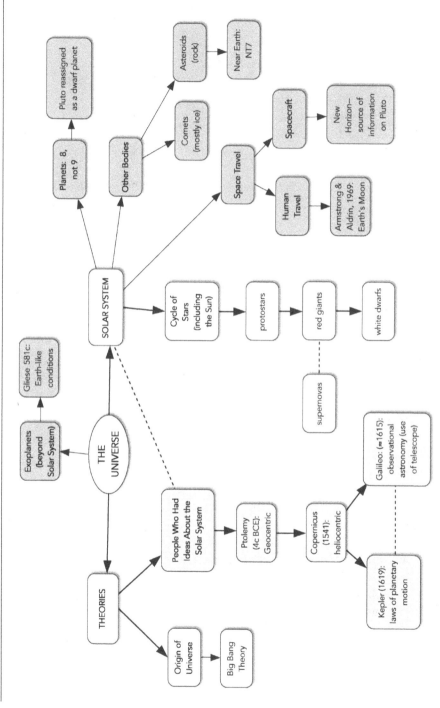

Figure 7.5. Examples of Informational Trade Books: Grades 4 and 5

Music

- *Trombone Shorty* (Andrews, 2015)
- *John's Secret Dreams: The John Lennon Story* (Rappaport, 2004)
- *Saint-Saens's Danse Macabre* (Celenza, 2013)

Dance

- *Footwork: The Story of Fred and Adele Astaire* (Orgill, 2007)
- *Alvin Ailey* (Pinkney, 1995)
- *Danza! Amalia Hernández and the El Ballet Folklorico de Mexico* (Tonatiuh, 2017)

Art

- *Diego Rivera: An Artist for the People* (Rubin, 2013)
- *Edward Hopper Paints His World* (Burleigh, 2014)
- *Through Georgia's Eyes* (Rodriguez, 2006)

Architecture

- *Round Buildings, Square Buildings, and Buildings That Wiggle Like a Fish* (Isaacson, 2016)
- *The Story of Buildings: From Pyramids to the Sydney Opera House and Beyond* (Dillion, 2014)
- *Under Every Roof: A Kid's Style and Field Guide to the Architecture of American Homes* (Glenn, 2009)

---

articles, and books for teachers over several decades. However, a common interpretation of the importance of background knowledge in comprehension has been the front-loading of content—when the teacher gives a preview of relevant topical information, including vocabulary, before students read a text. The assumption underlying front-loading is that readers cannot access new knowledge if they do not already have background knowledge. But this becomes a perpetuating cycle when students depend on their teachers to provide the critical background knowledge about a topic. When this happens, students simply are not developing the ability to independently learn from text.

From the start of reading instruction, students need to be taught to view texts as a source of knowledge. That does not mean that students receive texts on unfamiliar topics and are asked to struggle through them. Instead, teachers guide students by discussing how they might attend to the topic of a text and asking questions about their expectations of what content might appear in a text.

Devin's choices of small changes demonstrate ways in which teachers support students in using texts to acquire knowledge. Teachers can do much to introduce students to new topics, encourage them to broaden their choices, and deepen and share areas of expertise. Rather than being told the critical information to comprehend texts, students need to become adept at applying strategies such as predicting and asking questions about new topics. Students also need opportunities to reflect on what they have learned from reading. All too often, insights are forgotten if they are not revisited and reflected upon. Finally, creating occasions to share areas of expertise and interest with peers ensures that students participate in a community where knowledge is recognized and valued.

CHAPTER 8

Vocabulary and Text Complexity Systems

Example 1: Reba Jo loved to twang her guitar and sing while the prairie wind whistled through the thirsty sagebrush. Singing with the wind was one of the ways Reba Jo entertained herself on the lonesome prairie. (*The Horned Toad Prince*, Hopkins, 2010, p. 2)

Example 2: The Little House was very happy as she sat on the hill and watched the countryside around her. She watched the sun rise in the morning and she watched the sun set in the evening. (*The Little House*, Burton, 1942/2009, p. 2)

What level of reading proficiency would students need in order to be able to read the entire texts represented by these two examples? Is one text easier than the other? These are questions that are frequently on teachers' minds as they select texts for lessons and make recommendations to students for independent reading. Often, in making choices of texts, teachers rely on the text complexity labels that publishers have put on texts. Currently, the two most popular systems for text complexity are the qualitative Guided Reading Levels (GRLs) (Fountas & Pinnell, 1996) and the quantitative designations of the Lexile Framework (Stenner, Burdick, Sanford, & Burdick, 2007).

The answer to the question of the proficiency required to read the two texts above from the qualitative system of GRLs (Fountas & Pinnell, 1996) is that both texts fall into Level L, which is mid-2nd grade. Similar to the GRL system, the Lexile Framework evaluates the two texts as having the same level: 900 Lexiles. According to the Lexile Framework, however, these texts fall into the grades 4 to 5 range in the CCSS (NGACBP & CCSSO, 2010b). That is, each system designates the texts to be of equal complexity but the assignments of grade level by the two systems differ substantially.

The assignments become even more perplexing when viewed from the perspective of vocabulary load. *The Horned Toad Prince* has eight rare words: *Reba, Jo, twang, guitar, thirsty, sagebrush, entertained, lonesome* in a 35-word segment; *The Little House* has none. Yet in both systems, the texts are evaluated as equivalent (despite the quite different grade assignments made by the two systems). This chapter examines these two popular text complexity systems—GRLs and Lexiles—to consider how vocabulary figures into assignments of text complexity.

THE EVIDENCE

I begin by reviewing the treatment of vocabulary in text complexity assignments in the pre-digital age because the old system provided useful information about the vocabulary demands of texts.

Text Complexity in the Not-Too-Distant Past

Vocabulary demands of texts in the pre-digital era generally were established by comparing the words in a text with words on a list. Words were assigned to grade levels based on word familiarity and frequency (e.g., Dale, n.d.). Sentence length came into play in determining a text's readability, but the first step in the analysis involved matching words in a text with words on a prescribed list.

Results from an analysis with a pre-digital text complexity system—the Dale–Chall readability formula (Dale & Chall, 1948)—are provided in Table 8.1 for a set of texts. As the table shows, the Dale–Chall formula gives a grade level and the percentage of rare or infrequent words that are not on the designated list. As can be seen in Table 8.1, *The Horned Toad Prince* has six times the number of rare words per 100 than *The Little House*; the former is given an assignment of grades 5-6, while the latter is assigned to grades 1-2.

Reading teachers and specialists needed to compute the Dale–Chall formula manually, which was a tedious process. These manual computations, however, left teachers with insight into a text's vocabulary demands. Further, once teachers had conducted several manual computations, they had a good sense of what made texts challenging.

Currently, teachers are provided text complexity assignments based on GRLs or Lexiles, without information on challenging vocabulary.

Table 8.1. Information from Dale-Chall Readability Formula

Title	# Hard Words per 100(%)	D-C** Grade Level	3 Hardest Words
NARRATIVE TEXTS			
The Red Badge of Courage (Crane, 1895/2010)	7.0	HS	sinuous malediction imprecations
*The Horned Toad Prince** (Hopkins, 2010)	4.7	5–6	sassy blustery critter
The Little House (Burton, 1942/2009)	.83	1–2	tenement skating dumped
Zlateh the Goat (Singer, 2007)	2.5	3–4	gulden furrier feivel
INFORMATIONAL TEXTS			
A Night to Remember (Lord, 1955)	4.7	5–6	davit shudders hefty
Boy, Were We Wrong About Dinosaurs! (Kudlinski, 2008)	1.5	2	waddle tendons rhinos
Smokejumpers (Peterson, 2016)	2.3	3–4	retardant parachutist gulch
The Life and Times of Ants (Micucci, 2006)	3.0	3–4	pheromone mantises ramble

*Without Spanish words
**Dale–Chall grade-level assignment

As teachers view the assignments of *The Horned Toad Prince* and *The Little House* to the same levels in each of these systems, they ask, "What is the basis for these assignments?"

Text Complexity Today

At present, most published texts for use in schools and, often, trade books for children and young adults describe the complexity of texts according to one of two systems. One is qualitative—Guided Reading Levels; the other is quantitative—the Lexile Framework.

> *Teachers are provided text complexity assignments based on GRLs or Lexiles, without information on challenging vocabulary.*

Guided Reading Levels (GRLs). Human judges determine the GRL of texts, based on 10 text features (Fountas & Pinnell, 1996, 2016): genre, text structure, content, themes and ideas, language and literacy features, sentence complexity, vocabulary, words (number and difficulty), illustrations, and book and print features. Ratings for the individual factors are not reported. By that I mean that a rating is not given for the difficulty of the content, vocabulary, text structure, and so forth. Rather, a text is assigned a single level from A (easiest) to Z (hardest) that corresponds to kindergarten through upper middle school grades (Fountas & Pinnell, 2017).

Lower grade texts typically receive lower GRLs than higher grade texts, as can be seen in Table 8.2. But the information in Table 8.2 also shows that GRLs can vary greatly within a grade. Look at two texts that are often part of the 4th-grade curriculum: *The Horned Toad Prince* and *Zlateh the Goat*. The first is assigned Level L (mid-2nd grade) and the second, Level V (end of 5th grade). These assignments cover a large span—11 GRLs. Further, these assignments do not indicate why *Zlateh the Goat* is judged to be so much harder than *The Horned Toad Prince*. When considering challenging vocabulary (see Table 8.1), the difficulty is in the opposite direction from the assigned GRLs: Vocabulary in *The Horned Toad Prince* is more challenging in amount and kind than vocabulary in *Zlateh the Goat*.

In studies of GRL text assignments, the feature that best predicts the GRL of a text is the number of words (Cunningham et al., 2005). Many beginning readers may choose shorter rather than longer books

Table 8.2. Lexiles and Guided Reading Levels for 8 Widely Used Texts

	Lexile	Sentence Length (X)	Word Frequency (X)	Guided Reading Level	Typical Grade of Use
Narrative					
The Red Badge of Courage	910	13.91	3.55	Y	9+
*The Horned Toad Prince**	900	13.63	3.53	L	4
The Little House	900	15.14	3.73	L	2
Zlateh the Goat	920	14.77	3.63	V	4
Informational					
A Night to Remember	910	13.41	3.48	U	7–8
Boy, Were We Wrong About Dinosaurs!	910	13.44	3.48	N	2
Smokejumpers	.910	12.78	3.43	S	4
The Life and Times of Ants	900	12.63	3.36	Q	4

*Without Spanish words

for independent reading, but there are exceptions, such as *Green Eggs and Ham* (Dr. Seuss, 1960). With 783 words, *Green Eggs and Ham* is at least 10 times longer than the typical beginning text in the GRL system for Levels A to D. Further, many texts are divided into chapters, which students can read in sections. In fact, no text must be read in its entirety on a single occasion. No evidence verifies that the number of words in a text is the source of complexity for students.

Average sentence length is another feature that predicts GRL assignments (Koons, Elmore, Sanford-Moore, & Stenner, 2017). Average sentence length has long been known to predict text level (Klare, 1984) but, at the same time, sentence length is not a strong predictor of comprehension. In the description of Lexiles that follows, I discuss the problems with the sentence length factor in more depth and why it is not a reliable indicator of text complexity.

In contrast to sentence length (and number of words in a text), vocabulary knowledge is known to be a strong predictor of comprehension (Quinn et al., 2015; Sénéchal et al., 2006). Yet vocabulary fails to predict the assignment of texts in the GRL system (Cunningham et al., 2005). Vocabulary, the best known predictor of comprehension, is given insufficient weight in the GRL assignments of text complexity.

> *Vocabulary, the best known predictor of comprehension, is given insufficient weight in the GRL assignments of text complexity.*

The Lexile Framework. Quantitative formulas for calculating text complexity have been around for a very long time—almost a century (Lively & Pressey, 1923). As I described earlier, these calculations were performed manually until the advent of computers. The speed with which computers can process digitized texts spawned a new group of quantitative text complexity systems, the most prominent of which is the Lexile Framework (Stenner et al., 2007).

Similar to pre-digital text complexity formulas, the Lexile Framework focuses on syntax and word frequency/vocabulary. Syntax is measured by the number of words per sentence, similar to earlier formulas. But digitization changed the measurement of vocabulary.

When millions of words from texts can be retained in computer databanks, a word's frequency can be computed relative to all other unique words. The frequency of even obscure words (e.g., *davit, sextant*) can be established instantaneously. To get a Lexile, vocabulary is measured by taking the average of the frequency rankings of all words in a text. An illustration of how this works will help.

Here are the average frequencies for the words in the first sentence of *The Horned Toad Prince*. Note that the bigger the number, the more frequent the word: *Reba* (0), *Jo* (6), *loved* (132), *to* (25,580), *twang* (.7533), *her* (2,702), *guitar* (7), *and* (27,594), *sing* (32), *while* (606), *the* (68,006), *prairie* (22), *wind* (174), *whistled* (14), *through* (1,091), *the* (68,006), *thirsty* (7), *sagebrush* (1). The average frequency across the words is 10,777, which is the number of times that words such as *they* and *will* appear in English. But even in this single sentence, three of the words are very rare (1 or fewer appearances per million). An average frequency does not give an accurate sense of the difficulty of words in a text, because the high-function words (e.g., *the, and*) have such high rankings. The Lexile formula attempts to deal with this discrepancy statistically. But because the distribution of words in written English is sufficiently lopsided, the variation in the word frequency measure is small (3.36 to 3.73 in Table 8.2).

By contrast, the variation in sentence length is large (12.63 to 15.14 in Table 8.2), making word frequency/vocabulary less of a factor in predicting text levels than sentence length. To demonstrate the influence of syntax on Lexiles, I made simple changes to sentences in an extended text sample (1,000 words) from *A Night to Remember* (Lord, 1955). The type of changes to sentences is illustrated below where one complex sentence is changed to two simple sentences.

> **Original sentence:** Thayer thought of all the good times he had had and of all the future pleasures he would never enjoy.
> (Lexile: 910; Average words in sentences: 13.4; Average word frequency: 3.48)
> **Revision:** Thayer thought of all the good times he had had. He thought of all the future pleasures he would never enjoy.
> (Lexile: 560; Average words in sentences: 7.9; Average word frequency: 3.48)

The measure for word frequency/vocabulary stayed the same since the revision kept all of the rare vocabulary. However, the average sentence length decreased substantially. Reflecting this decrease in sentence length, the Lexile declined from 910 to 560. Merely by changing complex to simple sentences, the assigned level of the text dropped from grades 4 to 5 to grades 2 to 3.

However, shortened sentences do not make the content of this text appropriate for 2nd-graders. Chopping up sentences to hit specific targets of text complexity is simple to do, but the relationship between sentence length and comprehension is complex. As ideas get more complicated, writers use clauses and phrases, which increases sentence length. But when editors turn complex sentences into simple ones to meet text complexity targets, texts are not necessarily easier to comprehend. In fact, evidence shows that shorter sentences can have the opposite—and unintended—effect. Chopped-up sentences can make texts more challenging, especially for poorer readers (Lupo, Tortorelli, Invernizzi, Ryoo, & Strong, 2019; Pearson, 1974). Short sentences tend to have fewer links between ideas, requiring readers to make more inferences. The challenge increases for young and struggling readers because they have a harder time with inferences. Splitting sentences can have the effect of increasing comprehension difficulty for the very readers who are assigned lower level texts.

Current Text Complexity Systems and Beyond

Teachers' expertise will always be needed in determining which texts are appropriate for their students. They can be aided in making choices about texts by information from current text complexity systems. But, as the review of GRLs and Lexiles has shown, teachers should be cautious in assuming that assignments by these text complexity systems are sufficient for supporting their students' growth as readers. Current text complexity systems can be a source for some insights but gaps also exist.

Know the strengths of current text complexity systems. Both current text complexity systems give a general sense of where texts fall on a spectrum of text complexity. Higher GRLs or Lexiles typically mean that texts have longer sentences, which in turn reflects the likely presence of phrases or clauses. Knowing that higher text level assignments likely mean longer sentences can be useful in designing lessons. For example, a 2nd-grade teacher looking at the Lexile of *The Little House*—900—will expect that some sentences in this text are longer than the usual sentences in 2nd-grade texts. Consider, for example, this sentence from *The Little House*: "The man who built her so well said, 'This Little House shall never be sold for gold or silver and she will live to see our great-great-grandchildren's great-great-grandchildren living in her'" (Burton, 1942/2009, p. 3). The presence of the connector *and* makes the ideas fairly straightforward, but teachers may wish to direct students' attention to the unique parts of the sentence.

Similarly, the assigned GRL of a text gives insight into text and sentence structures. Texts at GRLs of A through D frequently have repetitive text and sentence structures, as in the classic *Brown Bear, Brown Bear, What Do You See?* (Martin, 1968). By GRL J, text structures follow conventional patterns. Teachers can adjust their lessons with this information. They also can use data on length of text and GRLs to consciously attend to increasing students' stamina.

Know the gaps in current text complexity systems. Information from current text complexity systems needs to be supplemented by teachers. Neither Lexiles nor GRLs offer specific information on challenging vocabulary. Both publishers of current text complexity systems *could* provide this information, as was the case with the Dale–Chall (1948) readability formula. However, at present, educational organizations do not require publishers to include vocabulary summaries with their designations of text complexity.

When texts are sorted according to sentence and text length, not content and vocabulary, coherent vocabularies can be hard to develop. Consider some of the topics within the informational texts in Level J of a leveled text program (Reading A to Z, n.d.): the history of soccer, the geography of France, and Día de los Muertos. As would be expected from the disparate topics, unique vocabulary varies considerably across these texts. In the text on the history of soccer, students are introduced to *referee, penalty*, and *cleats*, while the text on France introduces *lavender, crepes*, and *baguette*, and the book on the Day of the Dead features *altars, cemetery*, and *skeletons*.

A new group of words for each text means that young and struggling readers never have the chance to apply their expertise with new vocabulary from text to text. They are not building a coherent knowledge base about any one topic, whether that topic is sports, other countries, or holidays. One of the subsequent suggestions for small changes will be to cluster texts by topics to support the learning of shared words and to develop topic expertise.

Recognize that neither students nor texts can be assigned a single GRL or Lexile. The creators of both GRLs and Lexiles offer assessments that claim to place students in texts that correspond to students' guided reading levels (Fountas & Pinnell, 2012) or Lexiles (Stenner et al., 2007). A 1st-grader might be labeled with a GRL of J, or a middle schooler with an 800 Lexile. The student with the GLR of J may be advised to choose books from the Level J bin; the 800-Lexile student might be directed to a particular area of the library for text selection. Even small-group instruction can be circumscribed by students' designation, as teachers meet with students at a single level or Lexile.

The assignment of a unitary reading level to either texts or students poses obstacles for reading development. One problem with these assignments is the lack of information on the vocabulary load of a text in either the GRL or the Lexile system. Vocabulary is the most critical variable in determining comprehension and in increasing students' capacity to understand increasingly more challenging texts. When a text complexity system does not give information on the vocabulary demands of texts, teachers are stymied in their efforts to increase students' vocabulary prowess.

A second problem with putting a label on students as readers for extended periods of time has to do with the effects on students' views of themselves as readers (Hiebert, 1983). Students who recognize they are in the lower reading echelons of their class doubt their competence as readers. Teachers and parents also may evaluate students' capabilities based on these assignments. The specter of unintended consequences of placing students in groups does not mean an elimination of small-group work in classrooms. Small groups are a necessity if teachers are to provide the specificity and the support that students need. The issue is the criteria for forming groups, and the labeling and longevity of those groups. Small-group instruction needs to be oriented around specific goals (e.g., learning how rare vocabulary works in narrative texts) and for specific periods of time (e.g., a two-week period). Most important, these goals and intended periods of time need to be communicated to students.

Single GRLs or Lexiles for texts don't work, either. The assignment of a single level or Lexile to a text leaves the impression that the difficulty of a text remains static. However, the first chapter or the first paragraph of an article usually will be the most difficult part of the text to navigate. Using the colloquial language of soldiers in mid-19th-century America, the first chapter of *The Red Badge of Courage* immerses readers in a young private's thoughts about warfare. Although many contemporary American students may be challenged by the dialogue style, they can expect to gain momentum as they move through the book. The start-up of many books will not be as arduous as that of *The Red Badge of Courage*, but the development of context and primary characters is a signature of the beginning of narratives. A single assignment of text complexity fails to communicate to teachers and students the manner in which the text itself serves to create the background knowledge for comprehension.

SMALL CHANGES = BIG RESULTS

Naomi has made text complexity the centerpiece of small changes in her 3rd-grade classroom. She has made this choice because 3rd grade is the first year that students in her state take end-of-year, summative assessments. Text complexity of assessments has been a topic in the state's media and in workshops in her school and district. Initially, Naomi worried that her students would not be able to handle the texts on the assessment because of claims of increased text complexity. But after she learned that the core vocabulary accounts for 90% or more of the words in any text and also about how rare vocabulary functions in narrative and informational texts, she knew that this information could assist her students in approaching new texts, including those on the state assessment.

Conversations

Throughout the school year, Naomi has talked with her students about their capacity with texts. Knowing that the first paragraph of a text often influences students' perceptions of text difficulty, she has held numerous conversations about how to approach the first paragraph. Naomi puts excerpts of texts on a whiteboard to provide grist for these conversations. Naomi's state has a website where texts from the summative state assessments of previous years are posted. She especially uses those, not because she believes that the assessment is the be-all and end-all, but because her state identifies these texts as representative of what proficient 3rd-graders should be able to read.

In Table 8.3, I have provided the first paragraphs of some released passages from the 3rd-grade Texas STARR assessment (Texas Education Agency, 2016). I emphasize that this choice of assessment passages should not be interpreted as an endorsement of state assessments, but rather as an acknowledgment that 3rd-grade assessments are one of the first arenas where students are completely on their own as readers.

When Naomi presents an introductory passage from a text, such as those in Table 8.3, she asks a series of questions:

1. Is this passage hard or easy for most 3rd-graders to read?
2. Are there words in the first paragraph that might make this text hard?
3. When you look at the title and the first paragraph, what words might you expect to read in this text?

Often, struggling readers are reluctant to describe what is challenging for them. Hence, Naomi has crafted the first question so that it moves beyond the individual student. After these conversations, Naomi asks students to write about how they act when they think a text is easy, hard, or just right. After one discussion, Naomi noticed that a

Table 8.3. A Text Set for Conversations with 3rd-Graders Around Text Complexity

Text	Excerpt
Good Question, Chowderhead	My name is Chelsea Chowderhead. A chowder is a stew or thick soup. My father says that our early ancestors may have invented chowder. I wonder if our early ancestors got made fun of all the time, too. For me, the last name teasing began as soon as I started school. So when my family moved to South Carolina, I decided that it was my chance for a fresh start. I asked my dad if I could change my name.
Jake Drake, Teacher's Pet	When I was in third grade, we got five new computers in our classroom. Mrs. Snavin was my third-grade teacher, and she acted like computers were scary, especially the new ones. She always needed to look at a how-to book and the computer at the same time. Even then, she got mixed up a lot. Then she had to call Mrs. Reed, the librarian, to come and show her what to do.
Teddy Bear, Teddy Bear	In the early 1900s, New York store-owners Morris Michtom and his wife Rose invented a new toy that would change the toy industry forever. They made a stuffed toy bear out of cloth to honor the president of the United States, Theodore "Teddy" Roosevelt. . . . The Michtoms sent one of the bears to President Roosevelt and asked if they could use the name Teddy for the toy. The president agreed to the request.

number of students wrote about how they got scared when they saw unusual names of characters and places early on in a text.

Naomi used these comments to design the next conversation about text complexity. She asked students to observe the potentially hard words in a series of released passages from the state's summative assessment. As is the case with the three samples in Table 8.3, proper names were prominent in the first or second sentences of passages. Naomi led a discussion of how to deal with proper names in texts, especially ones that are hard to pronounce. Naomi and her students identified specific strategies: They might assign a pronunciation to an unknown word or use an alternative word for the name of a character or place in a story.

Collections of Words

Students' identification of proper names as a potential roadblock in their reading led Naomi to organize a collection of words activity, which she believed would increase her students' confidence in independent reading.

In the collection of words on proper names, Naomi asks students to differentiate between proper names that are part of the content of texts and those that are names that authors have given to characters or places. For example, President Theodore (or Teddy) Roosevelt is essential to the content of the third passage in Table 8.3, since he was the source for the name *teddy bear*. But the author of the second text in Table 8.3 chose to name the teachers Mrs. Snavin and Mrs. Reed. In such cases, where authors have generated names for characters in narrative texts, Naomi asks students to add comments on the word wall as to the reasons why authors have chosen specific names for characters and places. She asks students to reflect on whether their view of or interest in a story might change if the author used different names for the characters or places in the story. For example, why might the name Ivan have been more appropriate for the gorilla in a classroom favorite, *The One and Only Ivan* (Applegate, 2012), than John (the English version of the name)?

Core Reading

Naomi is aware of the evidence that has been described in this chapter, specifically that vocabulary is not a driving factor in how texts are evaluated in current text complexity systems—whether qualitative or quantitative. The lack of differentiation in vocabulary from level to level has led Naomi to stop assigning her students to specific guided reading levels. Instead, she has identified a set of topics that are central to the curriculum (e.g., nature, animals, transportation, games/toys) and for which she has books in her classroom library. She has taken books within a particular band of levels (e.g., N to P) and sorted them by topic, as illustrated in Table 8.4.

Naomi has seen how, when texts with target words on a topic are clustered together, students develop conceptual clusters of knowledge and simultaneously expand their recognition vocabularies, as they encounter the same words and ideas across texts.

Choice Reading

The recommended reading strategies for a grade within standard documents are many, but rarely is anything said about students'

Table 8.4. Illustration of Sorting Texts: Growing Giant Fruits and Vegetables

Texts	Topical Target Words Identified by Naomi's Students
Giant Pumpkins (Fimbres, n.d.)	carved, compete, contests, create/creative, organic, transport
How Many Seeds in a Pumpkin? (McNamara, 2007)	pollination, varieties
Plant Reproduction (Senker, 2014)	competition/competitors, contest, organic, reproduce, transport/transported
The Pumpkin Book (Gibbons, 1999)	carved, pollination, varieties

self-selection strategies. Naomi recognizes that when students' choices of text represent a mismatch between their ability and the difficulty of the content—whether too hard or too easy—independent reading time is not productive. To support her students in making appropriate selections for choice reading, Naomi has initiated discussions prior to choice reading sessions on how best to select appropriate texts. Students are aware, as a result of conversations about the core vocabulary, of the number of likely challenging or unknown words that they can expect in texts. Naomi has taught students to use the time-worn five-finger rule, which involves selecting a page or two of a text (about 100 words of text). For every unknown word, the five-finger rule asks students to fold a finger. If, by the end of the sample, they have used up all of the fingers on one hand, the text is likely a challenging one. Naomi has found that the five-finger rule has supported her students in becoming increasingly more adept at selecting just right texts for choice reading—texts that are not so challenging that students quickly stop reading and look for another text, and yet not so easy that students have few opportunities to extend their vocabulary and knowledge.

THE LAST WORD

Current text complexity systems are not helpful in assessing or providing information about vocabulary—the variable that most influences students' perceptions and comprehension of texts. The digitization that has led to the vocabulary revolution means that the vocabulary of texts can be provided easily once a text has been evaluated qualitatively or quantitatively. Similar to the pre-digital era readability systems such as Dale–Chall (1948) and Spache (1953), vocabulary can be equated with the grade levels at which it becomes important. In other words, the publishers of the two popular text complexity systems have the capacity to provide information on the critical vocabulary in specific texts. Educational organizations—whether large schools, districts, or states—need to ask that this information be included when they purchase texts from publishers. If we are to support students in developing bodies of knowledge and related vocabulary, this action is essential.

CHAPTER 9

Different Labels but the Same Concepts
English Learners

Example 1: "I'm going to catch a crab today," yelled Sailor Paul. Soon his nets were full and taut, and Paul hauled them up on the deck. "Get away, silly squid," scolded Sailor Paul. "Don't sprawl on my yawl." (*Sailor Paul and the Crabs*, Paulson, 2000)

Example 2: The children are drawing pictures. Ann draws a green lawn. What's on the lawn? A little deer or a fawn is on the lawn. Ben draws a pile of yellow straw. What is in the straw? A fawn lies in the straw. (*Drawing Pictures*, Hiebert, 2019)

In the United States as we approach a new decade—2020—about 10% of our students enter school speaking native languages other than English (McFarland et al., 2018). English learners (ELs) may not have English labels for concepts, but they do have labels for concepts in their native languages. In the usual materials and approaches of English/Language Arts, ELs are asked to learn to read words for which most young children do not have associated meanings in their native language, such as *taut* and *yawl* in Example 1. Instructional demands such as those represented by the first excerpted text can intensify the challenge for ELs. Example 2 illustrates a text where students' knowledge of activities (e.g., drawing) and aspects of nature (e.g., animals, growing things) are the foundation for learning new concepts such as *fawn* and *lawn*.

Additionally, evidence points to strengths of ELs, such as their acuity in attending to the sounds of language, which often are not recognized in schools. This chapter develops a perspective in which strengths that ELs bring to language learning are the foundation for the design of learning experiences for those students and in which the focus is on transforming aspects of instructional methods that can serve as challenges to ELs.

THE EVIDENCE

Instruction always proceeds best when it builds on what learners know, rather than emphasizing the gaps and weaknesses in learners' knowledge (Schwartz, Tsang, & Blair, 2016). Evidence verifies several potential sources of strength that ELs bring to vocabulary learning in English. These sources of strength include:

- Metalinguistic awareness
- Existing labels for concepts in native languages, and
- Cognate knowledge.

Learning is deeper and more meaningful when the experience begins with learners' strengths than when learners are regarded as empty vessels or deficient. A strength-based perspective means that we as teachers are continuously aware that ELs have knowledge and dispositions that are the basis for literacy learning. The sources of strength can be used to address ELs' potential needs:

- Background knowledge
- Agency as readers.

Metalinguistic Awareness

Non-French speakers traveling in Paris will be listening attentively to announcements of place names to ensure that they get off at the right stop. Individuals in such contexts are displaying a proficiency called metalinguistic awareness. *Meta* is a Greek word meaning above or after. Metalinguistic awareness refers to the ability to reflect on language rather than to simply use language (Tunmer, Pratt, & Herriman, 1984). Students who speak a native language other than English often have a greater level of metalinguistic awareness than monolingual speakers (Lesaux & Siegel, 2003). This increased awareness of language is expressed in sensitivity to distinctions in sounds. To comprehend another language, a listener needs to be able to segment speech into individual words. ELs who have even a modicum of English facility have had to distinguish English words from one another to comprehend or produce English.

> *To comprehend another language, a listener needs to be able to segment speech into individual words.*

This strength in metalinguistic awareness is especially useful in learning to decode (Tunmer & Myhill, 1984). EL students as a group perform as well as or even better than their monolingual counterparts in decoding (Mancilla-Martinez & Lesaux, 2011). This statement often comes as a surprise to educators—and it is something that is not widely known. The evidence, however, indicates that many ELs become adept at letter–sound correspondences quite readily.

This ability to figure out letter–sound correspondences does not mean that students are necessarily off to a better start, however. EL students, especially primary-grade students, are likely not conscious of their proficiency and depend on their teachers for them to recognize this unique capability.

Support from teachers is especially critical when ELs are given texts that contain numerous phonetically regular words that students do not know (such as *taut* and *yawl* in Example 1). ELs may decode such words successfully, but they may have no idea of what the words mean. The resounding conclusion from research is that ELs profit from learning experiences that aid them in acquiring new labels for existing concepts (Echevarria, Vogt, & Short, 2016; Garcia, 2003). Texts such as the one in Example 2 allow ELs to build on their knowledge of green grass and baby animals to learn new words such as *lawn* and *fawn*.

Concepts About Familiar Objects and Experiences

On entering kindergarten or 1st grade, most students can produce at least several thousand different words and often many more (Segbers & Schroeder, 2017). Similarly, children whose first language is not English have labels for familiar aspects of the world. The difference is that their labels for these familiar features are in a language other than English. The words with which students refer to these concepts are often not understood by their teachers. Nor are teachers necessarily aware of the thinking that students are doing in their native languages. During a read-aloud of *Caps for Sale* (Slobodkina, 1987) students who are not proficient English speakers may be following along and telling themselves a story using words like *monos* (Spanish) or *con khỉ*(Vietnamese) to refer to the monkeys that are pictured in the book.

Cognate Knowledge

Students whose native languages are in the Romance group (e.g., Spanish, French) have an additional source of strength in becoming proficient in reading and writing in English. Their everyday language contains cognates—words that have close meaning and spelling connections to words in literary and academic texts in English. For the many native Spanish speakers in American classrooms, cognates can be an especially rich resource, as verified by Nash's (1997) identification of 20,000 Spanish–English cognates. Some of these cognates are technical words that have come into Spanish (and English) with inventions, such as *televisión/television* and *radio/radio*. But many of the Spanish–English cognates fall into the category of common Spanish words with a connection to literary and academic English words, as illustrated in Table 9.1.

Academic and literary language can be a source of challenge for ELs (Cummins & Yee-Fun, 2007), so explicit recognition of the potential resources of native-Spanish speakers' cognate knowledge should occur early in students' school careers. Further, educators need to be aware that, if students cannot read in their native Romance-based languages, these connections need to be made explicitly because the pronunciations of words can differ substantially between a Romance language and English. For example, when confronted with the English word *possible* [pronounced **pos**-uh-buhl in English] in a text, native Spanish speakers may not recognize its similarity to the Spanish word *possible* [pronounced po-**see**-blay in Spanish] due to differences in pronunciation and accent.

Background Knowledge

Throughout this volume, two themes have been repeated: (1) background knowledge is a strong predictor of comprehension, and (2) texts are a primary source for expanding background knowledge. The relationship of background knowledge and text can seem like a

Table 9.1. Common Spanish Words and Their Relationship to English Academic/Literary Words

Latin Root	Spanish Common Word	English Academic/Literary Words
frigus (coldness)	frío (el)	frigid, Frigid Zones: South & North, Frigidaire (fridge)
lavare (to wash)	lavar	lather, lathery, lavender (originally used as a bath perfume), lavatory
primus (first)	primero	prime, primate, primal, primacy, primary, primarily, primer, primitive, primeval, primogeniture, primordial
re (back) spondere (pledge)	responder	response, respond, respondent, responder, responsibility, responsible
terra (earth)	tierra	terrain, subterranean, terrace, terrestrial, terrene, terrarium
		phrases: terra firma (solid ground), terra incognita (unexplored territory), terra cotta (earthenware)

conundrum for teachers of ELs. What happens when students do not have appropriate background knowledge for a text? Should teachers engage in front-loading by providing information before students read? Yet if teachers do this consistently, when will students become sufficiently facile with texts to expand their knowledge on their own?

This apparent conundrum can be resolved by careful selection of topics and texts. When thought is not given to ELs' learning experiences, the challenges for ELs in comprehending and learning from text are increased. Example 1 at the beginning of this chapter illustrates a text that can create additional obstacles for ELs. Even with considerable explanation, definitions of *taut, sprawl*, and *yawl* will be difficult for young children to grasp. These rare words also will divert young readers' attention from the English equivalents of known words in their language (e.g., *full, catch*). In Example 2, EL students can bring knowledge about drawing and the outdoors to the text. They likely do not know the word *fawn*, but the definition in the text, the repetition of the word, and an illustration of the animal on the page support ELs' acquisition of the word and its meaning.

Another potential challenge for EL students is the traditional emphasis on narrative texts in ELA periods. Even with shifts to more informational texts in elementary classrooms, narrative texts can be prominent in read-alouds and choice reading. Often, in narrative texts, authors assume particular cultural knowledge on the part of their readers (Bernhardt, 2009). Cultural demands are illustrated by two narrative texts from a unit in a core reading program (August et al., 2014): *Wolf!* (Bloom, 1999) and *The Real Story of Stone Soup* (Compestine, 2007). Both illustrate the genre of twisted fairytales, in which roles of characters in traditional tales are reversed. In *Wolf!*, the farm animals are literate and not at all afraid when the hungry wolf visits their farm. In the second text—*The Real Story of Stone Soup*—the narrator, rather than the villagers, is duped in the making of stone soup. The humor of both stories comes from an understanding of traditional western European tales.

By contrast, the informational texts in the same program convey content in a much more straightforward way. *A Mountain of History* (Time for Kids, 2013) describes the height of the faces of the presidents on Mount Rushmore as 60 feet tall—about the height of a six-floor building. *Amazing Animals of the Mojave* (Pringle, 2013) describes why roadrunners are able to thrive in a hot desert environment.

The aim is not to eliminate narratives in instruction of ELs but to recognize how content, such as irony and parody (e.g., *Wolf!*, *The Real Story of Stone Soup*), challenges ELs. Often, educators can ensure the creation of appropriate learning experiences for ELs simply by recognizing that concepts of narratives that may look easy to native speakers can have pitfalls for ELs. Further, when teachers recognize that many cultures have versions of common fables and folk tales, they can ask students to describe the form of the typical tale in their native language.

Finally, like their English-speaking peers, ELs often will not have the background knowledge for new topics in subject areas, such as different kinds of volcanoes or the role of the Nile in ancient Egypt. Writers of content-area texts, especially textbooks, can be insensitive to the needs of ELs (as well as struggling readers). The amount of information on cell reproduction in a science textbook or on the climate regions of the United States in a social studies textbook can be daunting. Teachers can support ELs by highlighting critical information and giving students repeated exposure to ideas.

Agency as Readers

ELs have strengths that they bring to literacy instruction, but they also have needs that can be distinct from those of their native-English-speaking peers. Often the unique experiences of ELs are not central to school life, where the focus is on the background knowledge germane to academic

> School tasks can support student agency through opportunities to make choices in what to read and how to respond to texts, to collaborate with peers, and to engage in meaningful interactions with texts.

learning. When teachers ask students about background knowledge for a story related to zoo animals, ELs may wonder why their English-speaking peers know about okapi or bonobos and they do not. One explanation may be that some of their peers have visited zoos or museums, but perhaps some students have not had these opportunities. Discussions about the sources of background knowledge—including experiences afforded by texts—can support ELs in recognizing that their learning capacity is strong.

Agency is the construct that describes students' dispositions or beliefs related to their control over and confidence in learning. Students with a sense of agency take an active role in their learning. Students who believe that they do not have the capacity to be good readers will be less engaged in reading activities. When confronted with texts they perceive as challenging, these students may avoid reading altogether.

Conditions of poverty can influence students' school participation (Barr & Gibson, 2013; Edwards, Ong, & Lopez, 2007). At the same time, resiliency and what Duckworth (2016) calls grit can vary substantially across students in the same community or even family (Condly, 2006). Good news comes from research showing that school tasks and classroom conversations can be designed to increase students' attention and willingness to participate in school tasks (McRae & Guthrie, 2009). Higher levels of student engagement, in turn, are associated with higher levels of reading achievement (Guthrie & Klauda, 2014). School tasks can support student agency through opportunities to make choices in what to read and how to respond to texts, to collaborate with peers, to engage in meaningful interactions with texts, and, above all, to participate with relevant and worthwhile content (Swan, Coddington, & Guthrie, 2010).

SMALL CHANGES = BIG RESULTS

All of the actions for ELs revolve around the creation of literacy experiences where meaning is at the center. A visit to Carmen's 1st-grade classroom illustrates how the 4Cs are designed to support EL students and to ensure that monolingual English speakers in her class learn from and with their EL peers.

Core Reading

In selecting texts for EL students to read, Carmen asks three questions:

- What bodies of knowledge is this content supporting?
- What do students already know that could be an anchor for this activity?
- What will students learn from this lesson that will extend and build their knowledge?

When Carmen applied these three questions to the decodable text series (represented in Example 1 at the beginning of this chapter), she knew that she could *not* use these texts with her EL students. Her choice was to cluster together available leveled texts and trade books according to topics, similar to the process described in the previous chapter. For the first part of the year, she used the texts and topics from *BeginningReads* (a set of free downloadable texts from TextProject.org). Carmen found the materials that accompany *BeginningReads*, such as picture and word cards (Cunningham & Hiebert, 2016), to be especially useful for word sorts and sentence-building activities. Carmen also drew on texts from other available leveled text programs and trade books in her school resource room and library.

Conversations

Carmen has seen that, by emphasizing words in new texts that students have encountered in previous texts, her EL students show confidence and willingness to be responsible for reading new texts. For example, in the unit on Animal Senses from *BeginningReads*, unique words such as *elephant, snail, bird, smell, hear,* and *move* are repeated across all nine texts of the unit. Carmen introduces each new book with a review of the words that students have previously encountered in the series.

Carmen also makes visible to her students the fact that their reading vocabularies are growing. She does this by periodically taking a text and highlighting in bold all of the words that students have seen repeatedly in previous texts. She then leads students in a discussion of their growing vocabularies and their capacity as readers. By the time that students got to the final book of the Animal Senses unit of *BeginningReads,* Carmen was able to demonstrate to them that they had encountered all but a handful of the words in the new text, *Elephant Eyes* (see below). She then moved the conversation to applying decoding skills in context to figure out the unknown words in the text.

> **The elephant is the biggest** animal **that** lives **on** land.
> **The ears and nose of an elephant are huge.**
> **An elephant's eyes are not huge like its ears and nose.**
> **An elephant's eyes are just a little bigger than your eyes.**
> **You can see** better **than an elephant. But you cannot** hear **things as well as an elephant. You cannot smell things as well as an elephant.**

Collections of Words

Carmen makes every effort to emphasize words for concrete concepts with her students. In so doing, she supports EL students in making connections between labels for these concepts in their native language and the English words. In selecting groups of words for the word wall in her classroom, Carmen relies especially on the open-access resource at TextProject.org called Word Pictures. This resource consists of pictures for clusters of concepts from the core vocabulary, including water, animals, the human body, metals and rocks, transportation, and money.

Carmen coordinates the focus of the word wall with the content of core reading. During the unit on Animal Senses, Carmen used the Word Pictures on animals for organizing the word wall. She began with the overview semantic map from the Word Picture set entitled Types and Characteristics of Animals (see Figure 9.1). Carmen adapted her word wall uniquely in that she placed the pictures on the word wall and asked students to post words in their native languages beside the

Figure 9.1. Semantic Map for Animal Types and Characteristics

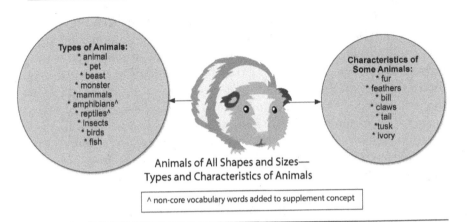

Types of Animals:
* animal
* pet
* beast
* monster
*mammals
* amphibians^
* reptiles^
* insects
* birds
* fish

Characteristics of
Some Animals:
* fur
* feathers
* bill
* claws
* tail
*tusk
* ivory

Animals of All Shapes and Sizes—
Types and Characteristics of Animals

^ non-core vocabulary words added to supplement concept

pictures. Carmen worked with students who were not literate in their native language to spell the words (making frequent use of a language translator on the Internet to confirm the spellings). Over the 2-week unit, students added words, pictures, and labels of animals and their features (both in their native languages and in English) to the word wall. ELs were especially proud of their contributions; monolingual English speakers enjoyed learning labels for words in other languages.

Choice Reading

For every core reading unit, Carmen makes certain that numerous texts on the focus topic are available in the classroom library. Carmen's interest lies in giving students the opportunity to develop areas of expertise and to use the vocabulary learned through core reading instruction in other contexts. She offers these topic-related texts as choices for students' independent reading, not as prescriptions.

Carmen found two sets of supplemental trade books that fit with the content of the Animal Senses unit from *BeginningReads,* which she had used for core reading lessons. Each book in the supplemental set *What If You Had?* uses cartoons to emphasize a feature of animals. For example, *What If You Had Animal Eyes* (Markle, 2017) contains cartoons of children with dragonfly eyes and lizard eyes and demonstrates their special capacities with these types of eyes. The second set of supplementary trade books, Animals and Their Senses, consists of books on the five senses, such as *Animal Sight* (Hall, 2005). This series lacks some of the comic relief of the *What If You Had* series but contains rich photos and information.

During the unit, Carmen also reads aloud two texts by Steve Jenkins: *Eye to Eye: How Animals See the World* (2014) and *Creature Features: Twenty-Five Animals Explain Why They Look the Way They Do* (Jenkins & Page, 2014). The latter text often leads to an art project because of the unique way in which Jenkins used paper collage in creating the animals' faces.

THE LAST WORD

Learning the most frequent words in written English, most of which are high-function words, often has been an entry point into English literacy. This task illustrates how ELs' challenges in learning to read efficiently and in a timely manner can be intensified by instructional choices. Dolch (1936) identified a list of 220 highly frequent words that research has shown account for a large portion of the words in texts—up to 50%. Conventional wisdom holds that, with the most frequent words handled, students should have a leg up in reading. This view, however, has some flaws, especially when considered from the perspective of ELs.

First, the letter–sound correspondences for vowels of a significant portion of the most frequent words do not fit the rules (e.g., *the*, *was*). Recognition of the word *the* will not transfer to other words such as *he, she, we,* and *me,* nor will learning the word *was* generalize to *as* and *has*.

A second feature that contributes to challenges for EL students when initial reading instruction emphasizes the high-function words of the Dolch list relates to the abstractness of many of these words. The distinction between the definite article (*the*) and indefinite articles (*a, an*) is not easy to communicate to young children. These ubiquitous words are essential for connected discourse but are not easy to define or understand. By contrast, concrete words are much easier to understand and remember—for everyone, not just ELs. In fact, learning a first language always begins with highly meaningful words such as *Mommy, Daddy, juice,* and *dog*. The foremost objective of reading instruction with ELs is for students to understand that written language involves meaning—objects, actions, and feelings—for which they already have labels in their native language. The use of concrete words such as *cat, dog, hand, ball, bed,* and *cup* does not mean that the high-frequency words are ignored. Texts for beginning readers can be written both to be meaningful and to give sufficient exposure to high-frequency words, as illustrated by the second example at the beginning of this chapter. For ELs, starting reading instruction with familiar concepts that are used in meaningful ways lays the foundation for successful English reading.

Children's Literature and Instructional Texts

Ada, A. F. (1993). *My name is Maria Isabel*. New York, NY: Atheneum Books for Young Readers.

Adams, J. (2009). *Lizard problems*. Columbus, OH: Highlights for Children.

Afflerbach, P., Blachowicz, C., Boyd, C. D., Izquierdo, E., Juel, C., Kame'enui, E., . . . Wixson, K. K. (2013). *Scott Foresman reading street: Common Core*. Glenview, IL: Pearson.

Aliki. (1988). *A weed is a flower: The life of George Washington Carver*. New York, NY: Aladdin Paperbacks.

Andrews, T. (2015). *Trombone Shorty*. Amazon Digital Services.

Angeleberger, T. (2016). *Inspector Flytrap*. New York, NY: Amulet Books.

Anthony, J. P. (1997). *The dandelion seed*. Nevada City, CA: DAWN Publications.

Applegate, K. (2012). *The one and only Ivan*. New York, NY: HarperCollins.

Armstrong-Ellis, C. (2002). *Prudy's problem: And how she solved it*. New York, NY: Harry N. Abrams.

August, D., Bear, D. R., Dole, J. A., Echevarria, J., Fisher, D., Francis, D., . . . Tinajero, J. V. (2014). *McGraw-Hill reading wonders: CCSS reading language arts program*. New York, NY: McGraw-Hill Education.

Balit, C. (1999). *Atlantis: The legend of a lost city*. New York, NY: Francis Lincoln.

Ballard, R. (1988). *Exploring the Titanic*. New York, NY: Scholastic.

Baretta, G. (2010). *Dear deer: A book of homophones*. New York, NY: Macmillan.

Baumann, J. F., Chard, D. J., Cooks, J., Cooper, J. D., Gersten, R., Lipson, M., . . . Vogt, M. (2014). *Journeys: Common core*. Orlando, FL: Houghton Mifflin Harcourt.

Beck, I. L., Farr, R. C., Strickland, D. S., Ada, A. M., McKeown, M. G., Washington, J. A., . . . Scarcella, R. C. (2008). *Storytown*. Orlando, FL: Harcourt.

Bloom, B. (1999). *Wolf!* New York, NY: Scholastic.

Brennan-Nelson, D. (2004). *My teacher likes to say*. Ann Arbor, MI: Sleeping Bear Press.

Brunetti, I. (2017). *Word play*. New York, NY: Toon Books.

Bulla, C. (2016). *A tree is a plant*. New York, NY: HarperCollins.

Bunting, E. (2006). *Pop's bridge*. Orlando, FL: Harcourt.

Burleigh, R. (2014). *Edward Hopper paints his world*. New York, NY: Henry Holt.

Burnett, F. H. (1911). *The secret garden*. New York, NY: Frederick A. Stokes.

Burton, V. L. (2009). *The little house*. Boston, MA: Houghton Mifflin Harcourt. (Original work published 1942)

Carle, E. (1994). *The very hungry caterpillar*. New York, NY: Philomel Books.

Celenza, A. H. (2013). *Saint-Saens's Danse Macabre*. Watertown, MA: Charlesbridge.

Christie, P. (2007). *Naturally wild musicians: The wondrous world of animal song*. Toronto, Canada: Annick Press.

Cleary, B. P. (2014). *How much can a bare bear bear?* Minneapolis, MN: Millbrook Press.

Collins, S. (2005). *When Charlie McButton lost power*. New York, NY: G. P. Putnam's Sons.

Compestine, Y. C. (2007). *The real story of stone soup*. New York, NY: Dutton Books for Young Readers.

Crane, S. (2010). *The red badge of courage*. New York, NY: Sterling. (Original work published 1895)

Cunningham, P., & Hiebert, E. H. (2016). *Teach your child to read and spell*. Santa Cruz, CA: TextProject. Retrieved from textproject.org/tutoring-materials/teach-your-child-to-read-and-spell/

Curtis, C. P. (2001). *Bud, not buddy*. New York, NY: Random House Books for Young Readers.

Dahl, R. (1961). *James and the giant peach*. New York, NY: Knopf.

Daywalt, D. (2013). *The day the crayons quit*. New York, NY: Philomel Books.

Dickinson, E. (1891). *The railway train*. Retrieved from www.cyclopspress.com/emilydickinson.htm

Dillion, P. (2014). *The story of buildings: From pyramids to the Sydney Opera House and beyond*. Somerville, MA: Candlewick Press.

Donnelly, J. (1989). *Moonwalk: The first trip to the moon*. New York, NY: Random House.

Dr. Seuss. (1960). *Green eggs and ham*. New York, NY: Random House.

Edwards, W. (2010). *The cat's pajamas*. Toronto, Canada: Pajama Press.

Edwards, W. (2013). *Monkey business*. Toronto, Canada: Pajama Press.

Elliott, R. (2010). *Laugh-out-loud jokes for kids*. Grand Rapids, MI: Revell Publishing Group.

Enzensberger, H. M. (2000). *The number devil: A mathematical adventure*. London, UK: Picador.

Erdrich, L. (2002). *The birchbark house*. New York, NY: Disney-Hyperion.

Fimbres, G. (n.d.). *Giant pumpkins*. Tucson, AZ: Reading A–Z. Retrieved from www.readinga-z.com/book.php?id=2113

Fletcher, R. (2003). *Hello, harvest moon*. New York, NY: Clarion Books.

Fowler, J. A. (2010). *What's the point? A book about multiple meaning words*. Bloomington, IN: AuthorHouse.

Frisbee, L. P. (1986). *John F. Kennedy: America's youngest president.* New York, NY: Aladdin Books.

Gagné, M. G. (2011). Paper. Amazon Digital Services.

Ghigna, C. (1999). *See the yak yak.* New York, NY: Random House Books for Young Readers.

Gibbons, G. (1999). *The pumpkin book.* New York, NY: Holiday House.

Gibbons, G. (2002). *Tell me, tree: All about trees for kids.* New York, NY: Scholastic.

Glenn, P. C. (2009). *Under every roof: A kid's style and field guide to the architecture of American homes.* New York, NY: Wiley.

Goodman, S. E. (2006). *Life on the ice.* Minneapolis, MN: Millbrook Press.

Gray, W. (1941). *Guidebook for streets and roads.* Chicago, IL: Scott, Foresman.

Greenes, C., Larson, M., Leiva, M. A., Shaw, J. M., Stiff, L., Vogell, B. R., & Yeattys, K. (2005). *Houghton Mifflin math.* Boston, MA: Houghton Mifflin.

Greenfield, E. (1995). *Rosa Parks.* New York, NY: Collins.

Gwynne, F. (1988). *A chocolate moose for dinner.* New York, NY: Simon & Schuster.

Gwynne, F. (1988). *The king who rained.* New York, NY: Simon & Schuster.

Hall, K. (2005). *Animal sight.* New York, NY: Gareth Stevens Publishing.

Hamilton, V. (1974). *M. C. Higgins, the great.* New York, NY: Simon & Schuster Books for Young Readers.

Hatke, B. (2014). *Zita the spacegirl.* New York, NY: First Second.

Henke, K. (2004). *Kitten's first full moon.* New York, NY: HarperCollins.

Hiebert, E. H. (2012). *BeginningReads.* Santa Cruz, CA: TextProject. Retrieved from textproject.org/classroom-materials/students/beginningreads/

Hiebert, E. H. (2019). *Drawing pictures.* Santa Cruz, CA: TextProject.org

Hopkins J. M. (2010). *The horned toad prince* (revised ed.). Atlanta, GA: Peachtree.

Howe, J. (2012). *Howliday inn.* New York, NY: Atheneum.

Isaacson, P. M. (2016). *Round buildings, square buildings, and buildings that wiggle like a fish.* New York, NY: Knopf Books for Young Readers.

Jenkins, S. (2014). *Eye to eye: How animals see the world.* Boston, MA: Houghton Mifflin Harcourt.

Jenkins, S., & Page, R. (2014). *Creature features: Twenty-five animals explain why they look the way they do.* Boston, MA: Houghton Mifflin Harcourt.

Keller, H. (1903). *The story of my life.* Retrieved from www.gutenberg.org/files/2397/2397-h/2397-h.htm

Kipling, R. (1894). *The jungle book.* London, UK: Macmillan.

Kudlinski, K. V. (2008). *Boy, were we wrong about dinosaurs!* New York, NY: Penguin.

Kuklin, S. (1998). *How my family lives in America.* New York, NY: Aladdin Picture Books.

Lawson, J. (2016). *Nooks and crannies.* New York, NY: Simon & Schuster Books for Young Readers.

Lloyd, J. (2013). *Murilla gorilla, jungle detective.* Vancouver, Canada: Simply Read Books.

Loewen, N. (2007). *If you were a homonym or a homophone.* North Mankato, MN: Capstone Publishers.

Lofting, H. (1920). *The story of Doctor Dolittle: Being the history of his peculiar life at home and astonishing adventures in foreign parts never before printed.* New York, NY: Frederick A. Stokes.

Lord, W. (1955). *A night to remember.* New York, NY: Open Road Media.

Markle, S. (2017). *What if you had animal eyes?* New York, NY: Scholastic.

Martin, Jr., B. (1968). *Brown bear, brown bear, what do you see?* New York, NY: Henry Holt.

McGovern, A. (1990). *The secret soldier: The story of Deborah Sampson.* New York, NY: Scholastic Paperbacks.

McNamara, M. (2007). *How many seeds in a pumpkin?* Toronto, Canada: Schwartz & Wade Books.

Medearis, A. (1997). *Annie's gifts.* East Orange, NJ: Just Us Books.

Micucci, C. (2006). *The life and times of ants.* Boston, MA: Houghton Mifflin Harcourt Books for Young Readers.

Montgomery, L. M. (1908). *Anne of Green Gables.* Project Gutenberg. Retrieved from www.gutenberg.org/files/45/45-h/45-h.htm#link2HCH0006

Muldrow, D. (2016). *We planted a tree.* Decorah, IA: Dragonfly Books.

Musgrave, R. (2004). Daddy day care: Antarctica's ultimate stay-at-home dads. Retrieved from www.doe.k12.de.us/cms/lib/DE01922744/Centricity/Domain/111/NAEP_2011_Rdg_Gr4_Released.pdf

Orgill, R. (2007). *Footwork: The story of Fred and Adele Astaire.* Somerville, MA: Candlewick Press.

Parish, P., & Parish, H. (1963). *Amelia Bedelia.* New York, NY: HarperCollins.

Park, L. S. (2016). *Yaks yak.* Boston, MA: Clarion Books.

Paulson, T. (2000). *Sailor Paul and the crabs.* Columbus, OH: SRA Reading.

Peterson, J. (2016). *Smokejumpers: Fighting fires from the sky.* North Mankato, MN: Capstone Publishing.

Pinkney, A. (1995). *Alvin Ailey.* New York, NY: Disney-Hyperion.

Pringle, L. (2013). *Amazing animals of the Mojave.* New York, NY: TIME.

Rappaport, D. (2004). *John's secret dreams: The John Lennon story.* New York, NY: Disney-Hyperion.

Reading A–Z. (n.d.). *Leveled books.* Tucson, AZ: Author. Retrieved from www.readinga-z.com

Rodriguez, R. V. (2006). *Through Georgia's eyes.* New York, NY: Henry Holt.

Roth, S. (2001). *Happy birthday, Mr. Kang.* Washington, DC: National Geographic Society.

Rubin, S. G. (2013). *Diego Rivera: An artist for the people.* New York, NY: Harry N. Abrams.

Schotter, R. (2006). *Mama, I'll give you the world*. New York, NY: Schwartz & Wade Books.

Scieszka, J. (1998). *The knights of the kitchen table*. New York, NY: Penguin Group.

Senker, C. (2014). *Plant reproduction: How do you grow a giant pumpkin?* London, UK: Raintree.

Simon, S. (2006). *Volcanoes*. New York, NY: HarperCollins.

Singer, I. B. (2007). *Zlateh the goat*. New York, NY: HarperCollins.

Slobodkina, E. (1987). *Caps for sale*. New York, NY: HarperCollins.

Smith, N. (2007, October 29). Unwrapping the past. *Scholastic News*.

Spinner, S. (2011). *Aliens for breakfast*. New York, NY: Random House Books for Young Readers.

Spyri, J. (1881). *Heidi*. Project Gutenberg. Retrieved from www.gutenberg.org/cache/epub/1448/pg1448-images.html

Tabor, N. (2000). *Ve lo que dices/See what you say*. Watertown, MA: Charlesbridge.

Terban, M. (2006). *Scholastic dictionary of idioms*. New York, NY: Scholastic.

Terban, M. (2007a). *Eight ate: A feast of homonym riddles*. Boston, MA: HMH Books for Young Readers.

Terban, M. (2007b). *In a pickle and other funny idioms*. Boston, MA. HMH Books for Young Readers.

Texas Education Agency. (2016). *STARR released test questions: Grade 3*. Retrieved from tea.texas.gov/student.assessment/STAAR_Released_Test_Questions/

Time for Kids. (2013). *A mountain of history*. New York, NY: TIME.

Tonatiuh, D. (2017). Danza! Amalia Hernández and the El Ballet Folklorico de Mexico. Dreamscape Media.

Udry, J. M. (1987). *A tree is nice*. Logan, IA: Perfection Learning Corporation.

Viola, H. J., Bednarz, S. W., Cortés, C. E., Jennings, C. J., Schug, M. C., & White, C. S. (2009). *Houghton Mifflin social studies*. Boston, MA: Houghton Mifflin.

Weeks, S. (2007). *If I were a lion*. New York, NY: Atheneum Books for Young Readers.

White, E. B. (1952). *Charlotte's web*. New York, NY: Harper & Brothers.

Winter, J. (2008). *Wangari's trees of peace*. Orlando, FL: Harcourt.

Wood, A. (1982). *Quick as a cricket*. New York, NY: Child's Play International.

Yolen, J. (1987). *Owl moon*. New York, NY: Philomel Books.

Zeltser, D. (2016). *Lug, blast from the north*. Seattle, WA: Amazon Digital Services.

References

Ahmed, Y., Francis, D. J., York, M., Fletcher, J. M., Barnes, M., & Kulesz, P. (2016). Validation of the direct and inferential mediation (DIME) model of reading comprehension in grades 7 through 12. *Contemporary Educational Psychology, 44*, 68–82.

Alexander, P. A., Kulikowich, J. M., & Schulze, S. K. (1994). How subject-matter knowledge affects recall and interest. *American Educational Research Journal, 31*(2), 313–337.

Anglin, J. M. (1993). Vocabulary development: A morphological analysis. *Monographs of the Society for Research in Child Development*, pp. i–186.

Barber, C., Beal, J. C., & Shaw, P. A. (2009). *The English language: A historical introduction* (2nd ed.). New York, NY: Cambridge University Press.

Barr, R. D., & Gibson, E. L. (2013). *Building a culture of hope: Enriching schools with optimism and opportunity*. Bloomington, IN: Solution Tree Press.

Baugh, A. C., & Cable, T. (2012). *A history of the English language* (6th ed.). New York, NY: Routledge.

Bernhardt, E. (2009). Increasing reading opportunities for English language learners. In E. H. (Ed.), *Reading more, reading better* (pp. 190–209). New York, NY: Guilford Press.

Biber, D., & Conrad, S. (2016). *Variation in English: Multi-dimensional studies*. New York, NY: Routledge.

Blachowicz, C., & Fisher, P. (2006). *Teaching vocabulary in all classrooms* (3rd ed.). Upper Saddle River, NJ: Pearson Merrill Prentice Hall.

Bloomfield, L., & Barnhart, C. L. (1961). *Let's read: A linguistic approach* (Vol. 3). Detroit, MI: Wayne State University Press.

Brenner, D., & Hiebert, E. H. (2010). If I follow the teachers' editions, isn't that enough? Analyzing reading volume in six core reading programs. *The Elementary School Journal, 110*(3), 347–363.

Bryk, A. S., Gomez, L. M., Grunow, A., & LeMahieu, P. G. (2015). *Learning to improve: How America's schools can get better at getting better*. Cambridge, MA: Harvard Education Press.

Brysbaert, M., Warriner, A. B., & Kuperman, V. (2014). Concreteness ratings for 40 thousand generally known English word lemmas. *Behavior Research Methods, 46*(3), 904–911.

Bryson, B. (2001). *The mother tongue: English and how it got that way*. New York, NY: William Morrow Paperbacks.

Bryson, B. (2015). *Made in America: An informal history of the English language in the United States*. New York, NY: William Morrow Paperbacks.

Calfee, R. C., & Drum, P. (1986). Research on teaching reading. In M. C. Wittrock (Ed.), *Handbook of research on teaching* (3rd ed., pp. 804–849). New York, NY: Macmillan.

Cervetti, G. N., Hiebert, E. H., Pearson, P. D., & McClung, N. A. (2015). Factors that influence the difficulty of science words. *Journal of Literacy Research, 47*(2), 153–185.

Chabris, C., & Simons, D. (2011). *The invisible gorilla: How our intuitions deceive us*. New York, NY: Harmony.

Condly, S. J. (2006). Resilience in children: A review of literature with implications for education. *Urban Education, 41*(3), 211–236.

Coxhead, A. (2000). A new academic word list. *TESOL Quarterly, 34*(2), 213–238.

Crystal, D. (2010). *The Cambridge encyclopedia of language* (3rd ed.). New York, NY: Cambridge University Press.

Cummins, J. (1986). Empowering minority students: A framework for intervention. *Harvard Educational Review, 56*(1), 18–37.

Cummins, J., & Yee-Fun, E. M. (2007). Academic language. In J. Cummins & C. Davison (Eds.), *International handbook of English language teaching* (pp. 797–810). Boston, MA: Springer.

Cunningham, J. W., Spadorcia, S. A., Erickson, K. A., Koppenhaver, D. A., Sturm, J. M., & Yoder, D. E. (2005). Investigating the instructional supportiveness of leveled texts. *Reading Research Quarterly, 40*(4), 410–427.

Dale, E. (n.d.). *Familiarity of 8000 common words to pupils in the fourth, sixth, and eighth grades*. Columbus: Bureau of Educational Research, Ohio State University.

Dale, E., & Chall, J. S. (1948). A formula for predicting readability. *Educational Research Bulletin*, pp. 37–54.

Dolch, E. W. (1936). A basic sight vocabulary. *The Elementary School Journal, 36*(6), 456–460.

Duckworth, A. (2016). *Grit: The power of passion and perseverance*. New York, NY: Scribner.

Duhigg, C. (2014). *The power of habit: Why we do what we do in life and business*. New York, NY: Random House.

Dweck, C. S. (2013). *Self-theories: Their role in motivation, personality, and development*. London, UK: Psychology Press.

Echevarria, J., Vogt, M., & Short, D. (2016). *Making content comprehensible for English learners: The SIOP model*. Hoboken, NJ: Pearson.

Edwards, L. M., Ong, A. D., & Lopez, S. J. (2007). Hope measurement in Mexican American youth. *Hispanic Journal of Behavioral Sciences, 29*(2), 225–241.

Fogg, B. J. (2009, April). A behavior model for persuasive design. In *Proceedings of the 4th International Conference on Persuasive Technology* (pp. 40–45). ACM Digital Library.

Fountas, I. C., & Pinnell, G. S. (1996). *Guided reading: Good first teaching for all children*. Portsmouth, NH: Heinemann.

Fountas, I. C., & Pinnell, G. S. (2012). Guided reading: The romance and the reality. *The Reading Teacher, 66*(4), 268–284.

Fountas, I. C., & Pinnell, G. S. (2016). *About leveled texts*. Retrieved from www.fountasandpinnellleveledbooks.com/aboutleveledtexts.aspx

Fountas, I. C., & Pinnell, G. S. (2017). Instructional grade-level equivalence chart. Retrieved from www.fountasandpinnell.com

Garcia, G. E. (2003). The reading comprehension development and instruction of English-language learners. In A. P. Sweet & C. E. Snow (Eds.), *Rethinking reading comprehension* (pp. 30–50). New York, NY: Guilford Press.

Gardner, B. (2012). Habit as automaticity, not frequency. *European Health Psychologist, 14*(2), 32–36.

Gladwell, M. (2006). *The tipping point: How little things can make a big difference*. Sunol, CA: Little, Brown.

Goodwin, A. P., & Ahn, S. (2010). A meta-analysis of morphological interventions: Effects on literacy achievement of children with literacy difficulties. *Annals of Dyslexia, 60*(2), 183–208. doi:10.1007/s11881-010-0041-x

Guthrie, J. T., & Klauda, S. L. (2014). Effects of classroom practices on reading comprehension, engagement, and motivations for adolescents. *Reading Research Quarterly, 49*(4), 387–416.

Hart, B., & Risley, T. R. (1995). *Meaningful differences in the everyday experience of young American children*. Baltimore, MD: Brookes.

Hasbrouck, J., & Tindal, G. (2017). *An update to compiled ORF norms* (Technical Report No. 1702). Eugene: Behavioral Research and Teaching, University of Oregon.

Hayes, D. P., Wolfer, L. T., & Wolfe, M. F. (1996). Schoolbook simplification and its relation to the decline in SAT-verbal scores. *American Educational Research Journal, 33*(2), 489–508.

Hiebert, E. H. (1983). An examination of ability grouping for reading instruction. *Reading Research Quarterly, 18*, 231–255.

Hiebert, E. H. (2005a). In pursuit of an effective, efficient vocabulary curriculum for the elementary grades. In E. H. Hiebert & M. Kamil (Eds.), *The teaching and learning of vocabulary: Bringing scientific research to practice* (pp. 243–263). Mahwah, NJ: LEA.

Hiebert, E. H. (2005b). State reform policies and the task textbooks pose for first-grade readers. *Elementary School Journal, 105*(3), 245–266.

Hiebert, E. H. (2011). Growing capacity with literary vocabulary: The megaclusters framework. *American Reading Forum Annual Yearbook* [Online], *31*.

Hiebert, E. H. (2016). *New perspectives in learning vocabulary*. Hoboken, NJ: Pearson. Retrieved from schoolcontent.pearsoned.com/eps/schoolcontent/

api/item/a2b8a1d0-dacf-45b9-95f2-656fbb198bd2/latest/file/myp17/
myp17_g_shared/GettingStarted/assets/myPerspectivesFreddyHiebert-
WhitePaper.pdf

Hiebert, E. H. (2017). The texts of literacy instruction: Obstacles to or opportunities for educational equity? *Literacy Research: Theory, Method, and
Practice, 66*(1), 117–134.

Hiebert, E. H. (2018). Building background knowledge and reading proficiency: One article at a time. *Text Matters—A Magazine for Teachers.* Santa Cruz,
CA: TextProject.org. Retrieved from textproject.org/library/text-matters/
building-background-knowledge-and-reading-proficiency-one-article-
at-a-time/

Hiebert, E. H., & Bravo, M., (2010). Morphological knowledge and learning
to read in English. In D. Wyse, R. Andrews, & J. Hoffman (Eds.), *International handbook of English, language and literacy teaching* (pp. 87–97).
Oxford, UK: Routledge.

Hiebert, E. H., Goodwin, A. P., & Cervetti, G. N. (2018). Core vocabulary: Its
morphological content and presence in exemplar texts. *Reading Research
Quarterly, 53*(1), 29–49.

Hiebert, E. H., & Lubliner, S. (2008). The nature, learning, and instruction of
general academic vocabulary. In S. J. Samuels & A. Farstrup (Eds.), *What
research has to say about vocabulary* (pp. 106–129). Newark, DE: International Reading Association.

Hiebert, E., Scott, J., Castaneda, R., & Spichtig, A. (2019). An analysis of the
features of words that influence vocabulary difficulty. *Education Sciences,
9*(1), 8.

Hoff, E., & Tian, C. (2005). Socioeconomic status and cultural influences on
language. *Journal of Communication Disorders, 38*(4), 271–278.

Hogg, R., & Denison, D. (2006). *A history of the English language.* New York, NY:
Cambridge University Press.

Jackendoff, R. (1992). *Semantic structures.* Cambridge, MA: MIT Press.

Klare, G. R. (1984). Readability. In P. D. Pearson, R. Barr, M. L. Kamil, & P.
Mosenthal (Eds.), *Handbook of reading research* (Vol. 1, pp. 681–744). New
York, NY: Longman.

Koons, H., Elmore, J., Sanford-Moore, E., & Stenner, A. J. (2017). *The relationship between Lexile text measures and early grades Fountas & Pinnell reading
levels* (MetaMetrics Research Brief). Durham, NC: MetaMetrics.

Lally, P., Van Jaarsveld, C. H., Potts, H. W., & Wardle, J. (2010). How are habits formed: Modeling habit formation in the real world. *European Journal
of Social Psychology, 40*(6), 998–1009.

Lang, J. M. (2016). *Small teaching: Everyday lessons from the science of learning.*
San Francisco, CA: Jossey-Bass.

Leech, G., & Rayson, P. (2014). *Word frequencies in written and spoken English:
Based on the British National Corpus.* New York, NY: Routledge.

Lesaux, N. K., & Siegel, L. S. (2003). The development of reading in children who speak English as a second language. *Developmental Psychology, 39*(6), 1005.

Lively, B. A., & Pressey, S. L. (1923). A method for measuring the vocabulary burden of textbooks. *Educational Administration and Supervision, 9*(389–398), 73.

Lupo, S. M., Tortorelli, L., Invernizzi, M., Ryoo, J. H., & Strong, J. Z. (2019, March 6). An exploration of text difficulty and knowledge support on adolescents' comprehension. *Reading Research Quarterly, 54*(4), 441–584.

Mancilla-Martinez, J., & Lesaux, N. K. (2011). The gap between Spanish speakers' word reading and word knowledge: A longitudinal study. *Child Development, 82*(5), 1544–1560.

Marzano, R. J., & Marzano, J. S. (1988). *A cluster approach to elementary vocabulary instruction.* Newark, DE: International Reading Association.

Marzano, R. J., & Simms, J. A. (2011). *Vocabulary for the Common Core.* Bloomington, IN: Solution Tree Press.

McFarland, J., Hussar, B., Wang, X., Zhang, J., Wang, K., Rathbun, A., . . . Mann, F. B. (2018). *The condition of education 2018* (NCES 2018-144). Washington, DC: National Center for Education Statistics, U.S. Department of Education. Retrieved from nces.ed.gov/pubsearch/pubsinfo. asp?pubid=2018144

McRae, A., & Guthrie, J. T. (2009). Promoting reasons for reading: Teacher practices that impact motivation. In E. H. Hiebert (Ed.), *Reading more, reading better* (pp. 55–76). New York, NY: Guilford Press.

Miller, G. A. (1995). WordNet: A lexical database for English. *Communications of the ACM, 38*(11), 39–41.

Mugglestone, L. (Ed.). (2013). *The Oxford history of English.* New York, NY: Oxford University Press.

Nagy, W. E., Anderson, R. C., & Herman, P. A. (1987). Learning word meanings from context during normal reading. *American Educational Research Journal, 24*(2), 237–270.

Nash, R. (1997). *NTC's dictionary of Spanish cognates: Thematically organized.* Lincolnwood, IL: NTC Publishing Group.

National Assessment Governing Board. (2015). *Reading framework for the 2015 National Assessment of Educational Progress.* Washington, DC: U.S. Department of Education.

National Center for Education Statistics. (2017). *National Assessment of Educational Progress (NAEP): 1992–2017 reading assessments.* Washington, DC: Institute of Education Sciences, U.S. Department of Education. Retrieved from www.nationsreportcard.gov/reading_2017/

National Governors Association Center for Best Practices & Council of Chief State School Officers. (2010a). Common Core State Standards for English language arts and literacy in history/social studies, science, and technical subjects. Washington, DC: Author.

National Governors Association Center for Best Practices & Council of Chief State School Officers. (2010b). Common Core State Standards for English language arts and literacy in history/social studies, science, and technical subjects, Appendix A. Washington, DC: Author.

National Governors Association Center for Best Practices & Council of Chief State School Officers. (2010c). Common Core State Standards for English language arts and literacy in history/social studies, science, and technical subjects, Appendix B. Washington, DC: Author.

National Research Council. (2000). *How people learn: Brain, mind, experience, and school.* Washington, DC: National Academies Press.

Neal, D. T., Wood, W., Labrecque, J. S., & Lally, P. (2012). How do habits guide behavior? Perceived and actual triggers of habits in daily life. *Journal of Experimental Social Psychology, 48*(2), 492–498.

Nesselhauf, N. (2005). *Collocations in a learner corpus.* Amsterdam, Netherlands: John Benjamins.

No Child Left Behind Act of 2001, Pub. L. No. 107–110, § 115 Stat. 1425, 107–110 (2002).

Ouellette, G. P. (2006). What's meaning got to do with it: The role of vocabulary in word reading and reading comprehension. *Journal of Educational Psychology, 98*(3), 554–556.

Pearson, P. D. (1974). The effects of grammatical complexity on children's comprehension, recall, and conception of certain semantic relations. *Reading Research Quarterly, 10*(2), 155–192.

Perfetti, C. A., & Hogaboam, T. (1975). Relationship between single word decoding and reading comprehension skill. *Journal of Educational Psychology, 67*(4), 461–469.

Plester, B., Wood, C., & Joshi, P. (2009). Exploring the relationship between children's knowledge of text message abbreviations and school literacy outcomes. *British Journal of Developmental Psychology, 27*(1), 145–161.

Pugh, A., & Hiebert, E. H. (2018, July 18–21). *An examination of rare words in texts across grades and genres.* Paper presented at the 25th annual meeting of the Society for the Scientific Study of Reading, Brighton, UK.

Quinn, J. M., Wagner, R. K., Petscher, Y., & Lopez, D. (2015). Developmental relations between vocabulary knowledge and reading comprehension: A latent change score modeling study. *Child Development, 86*(1), 159–175.

Ricketts, J., Nation, K., & Bishop, D. V. (2007). Vocabulary is important for some, but not all reading skills. *Scientific Studies of Reading, 11*(3), 235–257.

Schwartz, D. L., Tsang, J. M., & Blair, K. P. (2016). *The ABCs of how we learn: 26 scientifically proven approaches, how they work, and when to use them.* New York, NY: Norton.

Segbers, J., & Schroeder, S. (2017). How many words do children know? A corpus-based estimation of children's total vocabulary size. *Language Testing, 34*(3), 297–320.

Sénéchal, M., Ouellette, G., & Rodney, D. (2006). The misunderstood giant: On the predictive role of early vocabulary to future reading. In D. K. Dickinson & S. B. Neuman, *Handbook of early literacy research* (Vol. 2, pp. 173–182). New York, NY: Guilford Press.

Sornig, K. (1981). *Lexical innovation: A study of slang, colloquialisms and casual speech*. Amsterdam, Netherlands: John Benjamins.

Spache, G. (1953). A new readability formula for primary-grade reading materials. *The Elementary School Journal, 53*(7), 410–413.

Stahl, S. A., & Kapinus, B. (2001). *Word power: What every educator needs to know about teaching vocabulary*. Burlingame, CA: National Education Association.

Stallings, J. (1980). Allocated academic learning time revisited, or beyond time on task. *Educational Researcher, 9*(11), 11–16.

Stanovich, K. E. (1986). Matthew effects in reading: Some consequences of individual differences in the acquisition of literacy. *Reading Research Quarterly, 22*, 360–407.

Stein, N. L. (1982). What's in a story: Interpreting the interpretations of story grammars. *Discourse Processes, 5*(3–4), 319–335.

Stenner, A. J., Burdick, H., Sanford, E. E., & Burdick, D. S. (2007). *The Lexile framework for reading* (Technical Report). Durham, NC: MetaMetrics.

Stevenson, A. (Ed.) (2015). *Oxford English dictionary* (3rd ed.). New York, NY: Oxford University Press.

Swan, E. A., Coddington, C. S., & Guthrie, J. T. (2010). Engaged silent reading. In E. H. Hiebert & D. R. Reutzel (Eds.), *Revisiting silent reading: New directions for teachers and researchers* (pp. 95–111). Newark, DE: International Reading Association.

Swanborn, M. S., & de Glopper, K. (1999). Incidental word learning while reading: A meta-analysis. *Review of Educational Research, 69*(3), 261–285.

Thorndike, E. L. (1921). *The teacher's word book*. New York, NY: Columbia University Press.

Tunmer, W. E., & Myhill, M. E. (1984). Metalinguistic awareness and bilingualism. In W. E. Tunmer, C. Pratt, & M. L. Herriman (Eds.), *Metalinguistic awareness in children: Theory, research, and implications* (pp. 169–187). New York, NY: Springer-Verlag.

Tunmer, W. E., Pratt, C., & Herriman, M. L. (Eds.). (1984). *Metalinguistic awareness in children: Theory, research, and implications*. New York, NY: Springer-Verlag.

Walker, I., & Hulme, C. (1999). Concrete words are easier to recall than abstract words: Evidence for a semantic contribution to short-term serial recall. *Journal of Experimental Psychology: Learning, Memory, and Cognition, 25*(5), 1256–1271.

White, T. G., Graves, M. F., & Slater, W. H. (1990). Growth of reading vocabulary in diverse elementary schools: Decoding and word meaning. *Journal of Educational Psychology, 82*(2), 281–290.

Williamson, G. L., Fitzgerald, J., & Stenner, A. J. (2013). The Common Core State Standards' quantitative text complexity trajectory: Figuring out how much complexity is enough. *Educational Researcher, 42*(2), 59–69.

Zeno, S. M., Ivens, S. H., Millard, R. T., & Duvvuri, R. (1995). *The educator's word frequency guide.* Brewster, NY: Touchstone Applied Science Association.

Index

Jennings, C. J., 33
John F. Kennedy (Frisbee), 80
John's Secret Dreams (Rappaport), 92, 96
Joshi, P., 75
Joshua (grade 2 teacher), 35–38
Journeys (Bauman et al.), 90
Juel, C., 77
Jungle Book, The (Kipling), 58

Kame'enui, E., 77
Kapinus, B., 3
Keller, Helen, *The Story of My Life*, 1–2
King Who Rained, The (Gwynne), 65
Kipling, R., *The Jungle Book*, 58
Kitten's First Full Moon (Henke), 69
Klare, G. R., 102
Klauda, S. L., 119
Knights of the Kitchen Table, The (Scieszka), 80
Koons, H., 102
Koppenhaver, D. A., 101–103
Kudlinski, K. V., *Boy, Were We Wrong About Dinosaurs!*, 100, 102
Kuklin, S., *How My Family Lives in America*, 80
Kulesz, P., 83
Kulikowich, J. M., 83
Kuperman, V., 33

Labrecque, J. S., 17
Lally, P., 15, 17
Lang, J. M., 8
Larson, M., 36
The Last Word
 core vocabulary vs. incidental word learning, 38–40
 English learners, 123–124
 English morphology in proficient reading, 53
 4Cs implementation, 20–21
 informational text vocabulary networks, 94–97
 multiple-meaning words, 64
 narrative text vocabulary networks, 80–81
 nature of, 10

vocabulary/text complexity, 111–112
Latin, 42, 45–47, 49, 50
Laugh-Out-Loud Jokes for Kids series (Elliott), 65
Lawson, J., *Nooks and Crannies*, 80
Lead words, 29, 55
Leech, G., 25
Leiva, M. A., 36
LeMahieu, P. G., 8
Lesaux, N. K., 114, 115
Letter-sound correspondences, 33–35, 115, 123
Leveled Books (Reading A-Z), 84, 106
Lexile Framework, 98–101, 103–107
Life and Times of Ants, The (Micucci), 100, 102
Life on the Ice (Goodman), 90
Lipson, M., 90
Little House, The (Burton), 98–102, 105
Lively, B. A., 103
Lizard Problems (Adams), 54
Lloyd, J., *Murilla Gorilla, Jungle Detective*, 80
Loewen, N., *If You Were a Homonym or a Homophone*, 65
Lofting, H., *The Story of Doctor Doolittle*, 58
Lopez, D., 2, 102
Lopez, S. J., 119
Lord, W., *A Night to Remember*, 100, 102, 104
Lubliner, S., 90
Lug, Blast from the North (Zeltser), 80
Lupo, S. M., 104

Mama, I'll Give You the World (Schotter), 80
Mancilla-Martinez, J., 115
Mann, F. B., 113
Mariana (grade 5 teacher), 49–53
Markle, S., *What If You Had Animal Eyes?*, 122
Martin, Jr., B., *Brown Bear, Brown Bear, What Do You See?*, 105
Marzano, J. S., 30
Marzano, R. J., 30, 88

Rappaport, D., *John's Secret Dreams*, 92, 96
Rare words. *See also* Vocabulary/text complexity systems
  categories of, 67, 68, 78
  core vocabulary vs., 35
  English learners and, 117
  in narrative texts, 67, 68, 69–76, 77, 78
  in small changes approach, 77
  in supporting development of narrative elements, 70
  from synonym networks with concepts known to students, 70–71, 72
Rathbun, A., 113
Rayson, P., 25
Reading A-Z *(Leveled Books)*, 84, 106
Reading GPS (TextProject.org), 37–38, 39, 40
ReadWorks.org, Article-a-Day initiative, 92–93, 94
Real Story of Stone Soup, The (Compestine), 118
Recycling words, 6, 56–58
  archaic words, 58
  books that illustrate, 65
  change in parts of speech, 56–57
  change in word meanings, 56–57
  defined, 55
  homonyms, 57–58, 65
  in informational text vocabulary networks, 88–89
  Internet impact on, 55
  small changes approach, 61–64
Red Badge of Courage, The (Crane), 100, 102, 107
Reggie (grade 3 teacher), 77–80
Remixing words, 6, 58–61
  books that illustrate, 65
  collocations, 61
  complex phrases, 59, 60
  defined, 55
  figurative language, 59–61
  idioms, 60–61
  in informational text vocabulary networks, 88–89

  multiple meanings of, 55
  small changes approach, 61–64
Renaissance, 46, 47
Resiliency, school participation and, 119
Review process
  archaic words in summative assessments, 58
  core vocabulary proficiency, 38–40
  National Assessment of Educational Progress (NAEP), 82–84
  nature of, 20
  text complexity and summative state assessments, 106–107
Ricketts, J., 2
Rime groups, 35
Risley, T. R., 27
Rodney, D., 2, 102
Rodriguez, R. V., *Through Georgia's Eyes*, 96
Romance languages
  French, 41, 42, 44–46, 48–50, 51–52, 55, 63, 114, 116
  Latin origins, 45
  Spanish, 23, 45–46, 61, 63, 64, 115, 116–117
Root words
  Anglo-Saxon, 42–44, 45–46
  French/Romance language, 45–46
  new, in narrative texts, 67, 68, 78
  in word families, 45–46, 49
Rosa Parks (Greenfield), 80
Roth, S., *Happy Birthday, Mr. Kang*, 78
Round Buildings, Square Buildings, and Buildings that Wiggle Like a Fish (Isaacson), 96
Rubin, S. G., *Diego Rivera*, 96
Ryoo, J. H., 104

Sailor Paul and the Crabs (Sailor), 113
Saint-Saens's Danse Macabre (Celenza), 96
Sanford, E. E., 98, 103–104, 106
Sanford-Moore, E., 102
Scarcella, R. C., 3, 5
Scholastic Dictionary of Idioms (Terban), 79

Vocabulary instruction, *continued*
  text-vocabulary relationship, 2–3
  word families. *See* Word families
Vocabulary relays, 21
Vocabulary/text complexity systems,
    98–112
  Dale-Chall readability formula, 58,
    99–101, 105, 112
  digital analysis in, 4, 5
  five-finger rule, 111
  Guided Reading Levels (GRLs),
    98–103, 105–107
  Lexile Framework, 98–99, 103–107
  problems of unitary reading/
    complexity levels, 106–107
  small changes approach to, 107–111
  strengths and gaps in current
    systems, 105–107
  summative state assessments and,
    107–111
Vogell, B. R., 36
Vogt, M., 90, 115
Volcanoes (Simon), 25

Wagner, R. K., 2, 102
Walker, I., 33
Wang, K., 113
Wang, X., 113
Wangari's Trees of Peace (Winter), 37
Wardle, J., 15
Warriner, A. B., 33
Washington, J. A., 3, 5
A Weed Is a Flower (Aliki), 38
Weeks, S., *If I Were a Lion*, 79
We Planted a Tree (Muldrow), 38
What If You Had Animal Eyes? (Markle),
    122
What's the Point? (Fowler), 65
When Charlie McButton Lost Power
    (Collins), 78
White, C. S., 33
White, E. B., *Charlotte's Web*, 54
White, T. G., 34
Williamson, G. L., 12
Winter, J., *Wangari's Trees of Peace*, 37
Wixson, K. K., 77
Wolf! (Bloom), 14, 118
Wolfe, M. F., 15

Wolfer, L. T., 15
Wood, A., *Quick as a Cricket*, 60, 79
Wood, C., 75
Wood, W., 17
Word bingo, 21
Word families, 6, 25–40
  concreteness/abstractness, 32–33
  core vocabulary. *See* Core vocabulary
  in English morphology, 50–52
  general academic words, 33
  high-function words, 32–33, 123–
    124
  implications for instruction and
    learning, 29–35
  key concepts, 30
  lead words, 29, 55
  morphological/orthographic
    relationship, 34–35
  nature of, 25
  number of, 28, 30, 55, 67
  other dimensions of word meaning,
    34
  rare words, 35. *See also* Rare words
  root words in, 45–46, 49
  semantic networks, 30–32, 71, 72
  small changes approach to, 35–38
Word frequency/vocabulary. *See also*
    Rare words
  high-function words, 32–33, 123–
    124
  in vocabulary/text complexity
    systems, 103, 104, 105–106
WordNet, 55
Word Pictures (TextProject.org), 17,
    36–37, 121–122
Word Play (Brunetti), 19, 65
Word reminders, 62, 63
Word walls, 14
Word zones, 27–28, 35–36, 38–39
Written language
  active readers, 54–55
  flexible readers, 54–55
  habit of independent reading, 52
  National Assessment of Educational
    Progress (NAEP), 82–84
  relative formality of, 45
  as scaffold for remembering, 17
  sound-spelling, 34–35

About the Author

Elfrieda (Freddy) H. Hiebert is president and CEO of TextProject, a non-profit that provides open-access resources for teachers. Her contributions to reading research have been recognized through awards such as Literacy Research Association's Oscar S. Causey Award and the International Literacy Association's William S. Gray Citation of Merit Award. She has published widely in educational journals, including *The Reading Teacher and Reading Research Quarterly.* Her previous books include *Research-Based Practices for Teaching Common Core Literacy* (with P. David Pearson) and *Becoming a Nation of Readers* (with R. C. Anderson, J. A. Scott, and I. A. G. Wilkinson).